THE STORY OF THE

CHANNEL ISLANDS

A SHORT HISTORY OF THE

CHANNEL ISLANDS

John Uttley

FREDERICK A. PRAEGER, *Publishers*

NEW YORK · WASHINGTON

BOOKS THAT MATTER
Published in the United States of America in 1967
by Frederick A. Praeger, Inc., Publishers
111 Fourth Avenue, New York, N.Y. 10003

Originally published by Faber and Faber, Ltd.
in London under the title, *The Story of the Channel Islands*.
Library of Congress Catalog Card Number: 67-11659

Printed in Great Britain

Contents

Illustrations

Maps

Acknowledgements

In the writing of this book, I have received help and encouragement from many quarters. I am deeply grateful to many friends in the Islands and elsewhere, to Island officials, to the librarians of the Guille-Allès and Priaulx libraries, to the owners of the pictures reproduced here, and to my wife, mother and mother-in-law.

Chapter 1

Prehistoric Times

From the depths of the waters that lighten and darken
With change everlasting of life and of death
Where hardly by noon if the lulled ear hearken
It hears the sea's as a tired child's breath,
Where hardly by night if an eye dare scan it
The storm lets shipwreck be seen or heard,
As the reefs to the waves and the foam to the granite
Respond one merciless word.

THESE lines of Swinburne were written of the Casquets, the dangerous rocks to the west of Alderney, and the feeling he conveys here is true of all the Channel Islands, Jersey, the largest with an area of about forty-four square miles, Guernsey, Alderney, Sark, and the many smaller islands. But there is a fascination and charm about these islands out of all proportion to their size. This fascination springs partly from the beauty of their scenery, bracken and gorse-covered cliffs falling steeply to the foaming seas below, sweeping sandy beaches, strange twisted rock-shapes on little promontories, narrow winding roads between steep earth banks, these banks covered with wild flowers in the spring, old granite farmhouses tucked away in little valleys, fishermen's cottages nestling behind the sand-dunes on the coast.

Part of the fascination comes from the situation of the Islands, rising as they do from the seas in the jaws of the great bay formed by the Norman and Breton Peninsulas.

Logically they should be part of France, and the French name for them is Les Iles Normandes. Jersey is a mere fifteen miles from the Normandy coast, Alderney is eight miles from the tip of the Cotentin Peninsula, separated from it by the sweeping Race of Alderney where the tides whip through at eight knots. Even from the Guernsey group of islands, Guernsey the farthest out into the Atlantic, with Herm and Jethou separated from it by the Little Russel, and Sark, one can see the French coast clearly on a fine day.

But the chances of history and the independent efforts of the islanders have kept the islands free from absorption by France and linked them with the British Isles for nearly a thousand years. This story is a fascinating one, with its record of rival attractions and influences, and the result is the island communities of today, modern and up to date in so many ways—airports, traffic lights, complex systems of commercial potato, tomato and flower growing, an electronics light industry, and much of the apparatus of modern tourism. Yet the patois of the different islands still survives, their traditions and superstitions are jealously maintained, and their laws and forms of government are largely unchanged from the shape they took on in the Middle Ages.

Their story starts in the days of the primitive Neanderthal hunters, in Jersey. There, in a craggy headland of granite, is a cave, La Cotte de St. Brelade, in which a group of the old Stone Age hunters left behind over ten thousand worked flints, greenstone hammers, human bones, and animal remains of mammoth, woolly rhinoceros, great elk, deer, horse, and other smaller animals and birds. There are no remains of this people in the other islands, so that it looks as if Jersey alone was then part of the mainland, possibly through a rise in the level of the seabed. It is certain that through the ages the level of the seas in this area has varied greatly. Raised beaches are visible in Jersey sixty feet above the present tide level, and at low tide in St. Ouen's Bay can be seen remains of a submerged forest, blackened stumps and branches. In Guernsey, too, at Vazon Bay there is evidence of another forest which once rose from the present sandy bay, and striking later proof is the fact that within the last two centuries the passage between Guernsey and Herm was said to be so narrow that at low water the rector of St. Sampson's only needed a plank to cross the channel to take a service in Herm's chapel of St. Tugual.

Yet, when the next prospective inhabitants, the New Stone Age peasants, moved to the Island area in search of settlements, it is believed that Jersey was still connected to France by a strip of low-lying country. Only later, possibly through some great storm, the evidence for which is their cooking middens suddenly abandoned and filled with blown sand, did the Neolithic Jerseymen find themselves cut off from the Continent.

These new inhabitants had primitive boats, dugouts or coracles, and it is with their arrival that the other islands came to be inhabited for the first time. These people, a Megalithic people, are often named the Iberians as they travelled north from Spain towards the Channel area. They were agriculturalists, with a comparatively advanced culture—they could make simple pottery, they could cut and polish stone, grow corn and grind it in stone querns into flour. They left their imperishable tools, their hammers and axeheads and stone knives, which have been found in the Islands; but they left a more striking memorial to their way of life in the doemens and menhirs. These abound, many of them unspoilt. Little groups of these people settled in some more fertile sheltered spot in one of the islands, building their huts, tilling their corn patches, gathering shellfish—the shells were left lying in great mounds which remain in places. They were a hardy, swarthy, dark-haired race. To survive, and in particular to survive in their chosen place and not have to move on and start again, they relied on fertility of man and soil and beast. To preserve this the spirits of earth and water had to be propitiated, and the great Mother-Goddess, the presiding genius of all growth, to be worshipped. Hence their main religious memorials are the traditions that certain springs had sacred properties, a universal belief which has survived the centuries.

Memorials, too, are the great granite passage graves and standing stones. The dolmens, with their lintels, their passages leading to the sacred chamber, were built as the burial chambers of the Chiefs, for only strong faith would make these early men drag the huge granite slabs, often for miles up steep places, and set them upright with cross-pieces, and then cover the roofs with mounds of earth. They hoped that the dead Chief, lying there safely in the chapel in the earth, would by the power of his spirit help their seed to come up again.

These burial chambers can be seen and entered, generally with bent head, in many places in the Islands. A fine dolmen is La Varde, Guernsey, which lies inside a mound on a hill there, looking out towards the rising sun. Within is a chamber thirty-three feet long by twelve feet wide, with great granite slabs as walls, and a roof of more slabs, the biggest of which is sixteen feet by ten feet.

More impressive still is the passage grave known as L'Autel de Déhus, at Paradis, in the Vale parish, Guernsey. The name means Goblin Barrow, a memory of old superstitions about the origin of these magical structures. Its mound is complete, grass-covered with ancient turf, and inside, as well as the main chamber beyond the powerful lintel and the heavy passage with its irregular stony walls, are other smaller rooms or chapels. On one of the capstones here is a carving, almost surrealist in appearance, of a human figure. A face, arms and hands are etched in, and beneath is a crescent-shaped symbol representing a collar with concentric loops, a strange and fascinating shape whose meaning has been forgotten for three thousand years.

The finest grave of all is in Jersey, in Grouville Parish. It is the Hougue Bie, Hougue being the patois for a mound. There in the forty-foot high mound a passage leads to a main chamber thirty feet long, with chapels on the north, south and west. In this when it was excavated were found lying scattered the bones of eight people, two of them women. Perhaps the great Chief had his wives or his favourite slave girls to take with him into the Unknown, or perhaps it became the family mausoleum.

Little else was found, for when the Viking raiders swooped down on the islands, they pillaged all the tombs. Not that they were the only vandals; F. C. Lukis, the pioneer local archaeologist, had a desperate struggle to preserve the dolmens and stones which still remain. It is recorded that when he explored the passage grave named Creux ès Fées (Fairy Cave) he found it had been filled with rubble on the orders of a colonel. The troops who manned the nearby fort, Fort Saumarez, were not as superstitious as the local people, and they took refuge in the ancient haunted dolmen when they were too drunk to report. So the commander simply filled the tomb with stones.

In Jersey, above St. Helier, the authorities were excavating for a drill ground, and they unearthed a great dolmen. This was voted by the Jersey States to be given to the Governor, Marshal Conway, who promptly had it removed to his country seat at Henley in England.

The saddest tale of all is that of the fine menhir on Herm, which used to look out over the Humps towards the Casquet Rocks, so cruel and terrible to mariners. The granite quarrymen pulled this down to take to England for a plinth, but it was too heavy, they could not carry it. So they broke it up, and the pieces went in an ordinary cargo of granite, much to the anger of the fishermen for whom it was a famous seamark, to give them their position in that dangerous sea.

These menhirs, or Longues Pierres, abound on the Islands, often grouped in the neighbourhood of a dolmen, or set to mark the boundaries of the stretch of arable land cultivated by the tribe or clan, or set overlooking the sea to ward off evil spirits or to frighten the raiders who might attack the little settlements. This power to avert evil was associated with the stones and graves for many centuries, as indeed it is in other lands. A legend about the Hougue Bie grave records that the mound was built by a lady of Hambye in Normandy, over the grave of her husband. He had come to fight a dragon lurking in the marshes of St. Lawrence. It is of course only a myth, although the family of Hambye from Normandy did own land at the site of the dolmen, and there is probably some element of truth in the tale.

The most exciting survivals from these Megalithic peoples are two statue-type carvings in Guernsey. One is a five-foot stone pillar with its top carved as a female head and bust, and the whole figure is like a huge woman. A row of small knobs like curls decorate her head, or it may be a chaplet. There is a slight drapery around her and her breasts are bare. She now stands as one of the gateposts of the churchyard of St. Martin de la Bellieuse, not quite in holy ground, but part of it. Her name is La Gran'mère du Chimquière, or Great Mother of the Churchyard. The pillar has been broken in half because the figure had the reputation of being an idol. She is certainly a representation of the ancient Mediterranean Mother Goddess; she looks with a sphinx-like stare at the people walking or driving down the narrow twisting road past her resting place.

She used to stand in the church cemetery, with a flat stone hollowed in two places to make shallow cups at her feet. As late as the nineteenth century it was the custom to leave an offering of flowers or fruit in these cups, and a churchwarden broke the statue for fear that her ancient worship was still continuing.

A second statue, possible older, is not so well finished as La Gran'mère, but it is more dramatic and sinister in its feeling. Again it is a figure of a goddess, with a strong personality and heavily carved features. It was discovered in the church of St. Marie du Castro, in Guernsey, where it was safe from storm and tempest. Now it has been turned out of the church, and it stands in the churchyard, near the west door, among the tombstones, a solemn dignified figure which makes the tombs

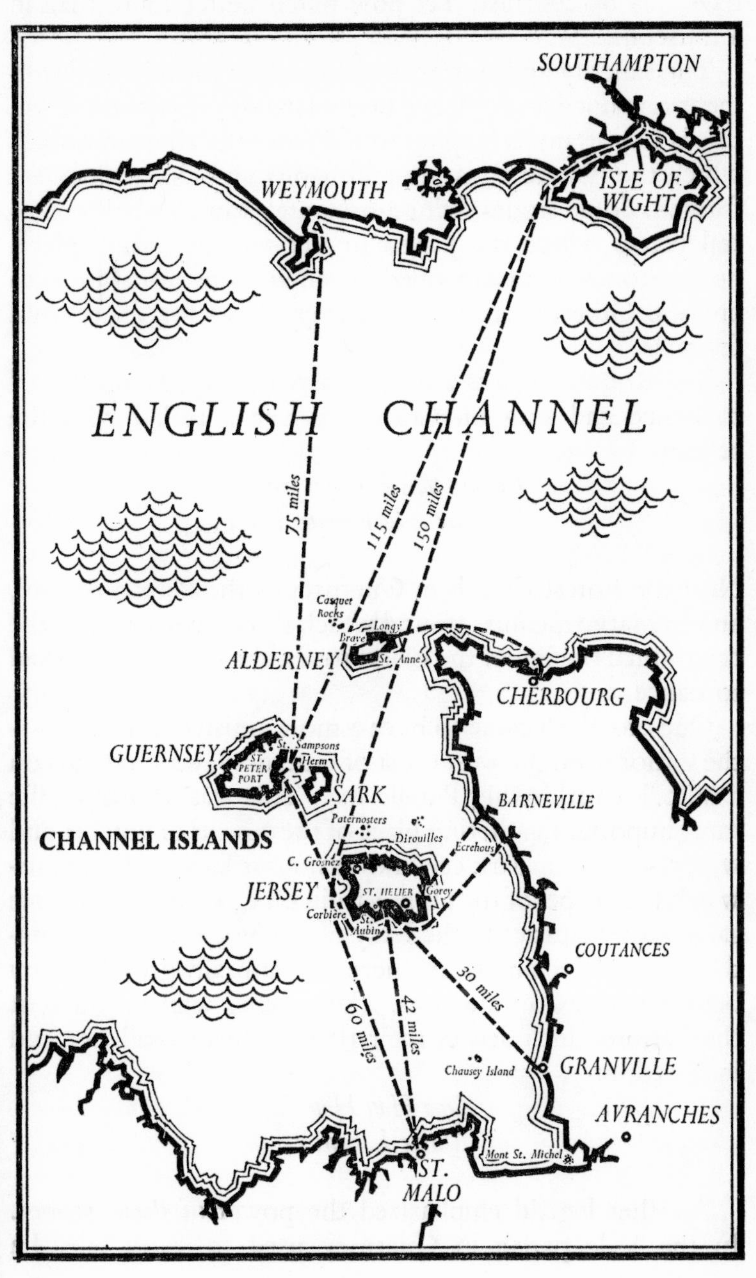
SOUTHAMPTON
WEYMOUTH
ISLE OF WIGHT
ENGLISH CHANNEL
75 miles
115 miles
150 miles
Casquet Rocks
Longy
Braye
ALDERNEY
St. Anne
CHERBOURG
GUERNSEY
St. Sampsons
ST. PETER PORT
Herm
SARK
BARNEVILLE
CHANNEL ISLANDS
Paternosters
Dirouilles
Ecrehous
C. Grosnez
JERSEY
ST. HELIER
Gorey
Corbière
St. Aubin
COUTANCES
30 miles
60 miles
42 miles
Chausey Island
GRANVILLE
AVRANCHES
Mont St. Michel
ST. MALO

B

frivolous by contrast. Yet how much better there than in a museum.

The sanctity and power of these statue menhirs and dolmens remained an influence in the Islands for centuries, and this is important as helping to influence the environment in which the islanders' nature and habits and characters were formed. Some stones, lying horizontal, came to be the central places where the parish or fief meetings took place. Some stones were sanctified by their transformation into crosses. Others were the gathering places for dances and festivals.

The Roque Balan is a stone where the peasants collected to dance and sing on Christmas Eve a ballad with the refrain:

J'irons tous à la St Jean
Dansair à la Rocque Balan.

Near the Forest church in Guernsey is the Perron du Roi, another large menhir, around which those taking part in the ceremonial tracing of the island roads, the Chevauchée, used to dance.

One cromlech came to have a more sinister connection—the Catioroc on the west coast of Guernsey, which stands on a hillock overlooking Perelle Bay. This was known as the most important gathering place of the covens of witches and wizards for their dark celebrations. As it faced seawards towards the chapel of the Holy Virgin on Lihou Island, a place sacred for centuries to the Lady of the Sea, where the Benedictines had a small priory, there was naturally great hostility between the two influences. The witches who gathered at the Catioroc included in their rites a defiant challenge and incantation:

Que Hou Hou
Marie Lihou.

Another legend emphasized the power of these stones. In the Vale parish in Guernsey used to stand one, La

Rocque qui Sonne, which when struck gave out a clear ringing noise. A local man, Hocart, ignoring superstition, ordered that it should be broken up and used as doorposts and lintel for his new house. As it was being smashed, the sound of the hammer could be heard over a mile away, but the work went on and the house was finished. The iconoclast was to pay dearly for his daring; before he could move in, the house was burnt down. Then two ships, in which part of the great stone had been laden for England, sank, and when the man retreated to Alderney, ill luck followed and his new house there was burnt down, too. Finally Hocart, in desperation, set sail back to Guernsey, but some of the rigging fell down on his head and killed him.

The impressive list of Megalithic remains in the Islands would have been much greater if Alderney had survived untouched by Government building operations in the nineteenth century. Unfortunately the very area where they chose to build their most extensive fortifications and barracks was that where most remains were reputed to be. Holinshed pays an earlier tribute to the island's archaeological interest in his Chronicles where he says: 'Beside this there is moreover the Isle of Alderney, a verie pretty plot about 7 miles in compass, wherein a preest not long since did find a coffin of stone in which lay a body of a giant, whose foreteeth were as big as a man's fist."

There were some surviving remains, the most important of which were Megalithic tombs, Les Pourciaux, above Longy Bay. Another was an enclosure at Mannez, of an area about a hundred yards square, by a double row of upright stones; these were perhaps the spiritual defences of a cluster of huts. At Château à l'Etoc were found great quantities of bones, the pathetic survival of a prehistoric cemetery. This gives some substance to a very old belief that the Islands were places of special sanctity and were used as burial places for the dead from the area of North-west France. Various old records support this. A friend of Plutarch's grandfather, a Greek named Sylla, reports that 'Guernsey was called Holy

Island, and the priests were accustomed to voyage from there to Delos every thirty years, and then to return, and often, although they were permitted to return to their birthplaces by their laws after having served Saturn for thirty years, yet often they preferred to remain in the tranquil retirement of the island.' Another Greek, Procopius, writing about A.D. 547, reported that Breton fishermen of an island subject to the Franks were exempt from all tribute, because they conveyed the dead into a neighbouring island. These fishermen came from Jersey, La Porte Sainte, and ended their funeral voyages in Guernsey, L'Ile Bienheureuse.

But the Islands lie on the cross-Channel route and can be reached easily by any skilled seaman from the coasts of France. Naturally it was not only undertaker-fishermen, or priests coming to retire, as so many others have done in later centuries, who made their way to them in the centuries B.C.

In Alderney on Longy Common there is evidence of a large bronze foundry, with a store of axes, sickles, knives, swords and spearheads. Among the spearheads were two with barbed edges, which were probably imported from Britain. In Jersey, too, a hoard of bronze weapons has been found; this shows that immigrants came from North-west France, for, as a tribe or clan moved from one settlement to another, the bronze-founders moved with them. In Guernsey, on the north coast, there were single graves, a sign that some of the La Tene Celts, with their distinctive pottery and iron weapons, had reached and settled there. These people left other remains, saltings and kilns.

Other finds, on an islet of the Minquiers group, of good black pottery, and a hoard of coins on a fortified promontory at Rozel in Jersey are good evidence that as the Romans brought pressure to bear and then attacked the Armorican tribes of Brittany, some of them got away to Jersey. Caesar himself admitted ruefully how clever these people were at fortifying a headland, and when Caesar's troops laboriously worked towards it, the elusive enemy took to their leather-sailed ships and slipped away to another point.

Incidentally, it is interesting how this evidence that Jersey received immigrants from Brittany, while Guernsey's newer inhabitants came across from Normandy, fits in with a strong local tradition today that the Guernsey 'Donkey' is a Norman and the Jersey 'Crapaud' (Toad) is a Breton.

The mistiness of this early history is not cleared much during the period of the Roman Empire. The Romans gave the name Unelli to the peoples inhabiting the Cotentin peninsula, which would include the Islands, and clearly officials from Constantia the tribal capital would pay periodic visits to collect taxes. But there is little evidence of Roman occupation. A few coins, handmills, fragments of pottery and a small stone carving are the only tangible remains, except for one spot in Alderney. There, overlooking Longy Bay, the original harbour of the island, is a building now called the Nunnery, with near by an area known as the Old Town. This building, a square fort with rounded corners, its stones cemented with brickdust mortar, and with herring-pattern brickwork, was almost certainly a Roman fort and signal station of about A.D. 350, built as one of Rome's defences for Channel shipping against raiders. It is similar in conception to the forts for the defence of the Saxon shore, which ringed the south coast of Britain. Naturally the inhabitants tended to gather round this strongpoint for protection, in the area of the Old Town. It is a desolate place today, for later great sandstorms overwhelmed it and other parts of the island, a judgement of God on the islanders, it was said, for murdering the crew of a Spanish ship.

The only other building which is almost certainly Roman is a small rectangular stone room near the Pinacle Rock on Jersey. It is thought to have been a subsidiary signal station, built to link up with Alderney; but other authorities say it was a shrine to the Old Gods, kept intact by a stubborn band of pagan worshippers at the time when Christianity was destroying their influence.

This site has added interest, as it has traces of human settlement for at least two thousand years. On the col which links the two-hundred-foot high Pinacle Rock itself to the land have been uncovered successive layers of remains. The lowest, in dark earth, showed a settlement with a number of definite hearths, with well-made pottery, flint, bone and stone tools, and some bones of domestic animals. In the gravelly layer above this have been excavated two ramparts, formed to make a small fortress on the col. The inhabitants of this period, too, have left their different remains, heavy dull-brown pottery, barbed arrowheads, polished stone axes, and a flat bronze axe. The layer above this, of dark sand, has produced evidence of settlement from the Late Bronze Age to the La Tene Iron Age, large storage jars, a burnished black bowl, and bronze spearhead. Finally, below today's turf, in the pale blown sand were found Roman potsherds, bronze rings, scraps of iron, an iron blade, and a coin of the Emperor Commodus, about A.D. 185.

Though the sum total of remains is small, and though after its period of greatness from A.D. 69 to A.D. 180 the Roman power declined, so that these Islands on its perimeter were little affected by it, yet it must have left behind among the islanders a memory of a more civilized way of life. The villas or estates of the Gallo-Roman lordlings are still recalled by the suffix-ville in many island place names—such as Leoville, Anneville.

The Roman ways destroyed too the dreadful power of Druidism, the official religion of the Celts, with its human sacrifices and sacred groves, which must have had some influence in the Islands however strongly the inhabitants clung to their older less fearful faith. Rome's third bequest was probably the most important and far-reaching, the tradition of Roman Law, a tradition handed down in spite of all the destruction and havoc of the following centuries to be a basis of the Islands' legal system ever since.

In 486 the Franks, who had been gradually breaking down the Roman control of northern France, won, under their leader Clovis, a final victory over the Roman general, Syagrius. The Roman power was finished. The islanders were left to eke out their precarious living on the edge of the known world, a lawless and dangerous world where the old master had gone and no one knew from where the next would come sweeping down.

Chapter 2

Saints and Sea-Raiders

ONLY one tenuous link remained with civilization, the Christian link, for which there is some evidence from the names of parish churches in Jersey and Guernsey. St. Martin of Tours was the driving force behind Christian missionary expansion north-westward as early as the end of the fourth century, and it may be assumed that he and his successors influenced the islands by the fifth century.

The first recorded invaders after this time were also good, not evil, supplementing, if rivalling, the work of the earlier unknown missionaries. Although the Frankish-German occupation of France spread fast after Clovis, and in the allotment of territory Neustria (Normandy) was given to Childebert, he and his brothers were so busy fighting each other that they had little time for remote islands. Yet indirectly they had an important influence. Their wild forces had devastated a large part of Armorica (Brittany), and left it depopulated. News of this spare land reached the Christian leaders in west Britain, who were hard pressed by the Anglo-Saxons, and they with their bishops and priests set out for this possible refuge. It is a fair guess that some of them put in at the islands as they sailed south, and certainly St. Sampson, who was to return later, gathered a force from them, 'as the inhabitants were well known to him', to support him in a Breton clan struggle.

After establishing themselves in Brittany, these Christian missionaries returned to convert the islanders. The first of the heroic band to make the dangerous sea crossing was St.

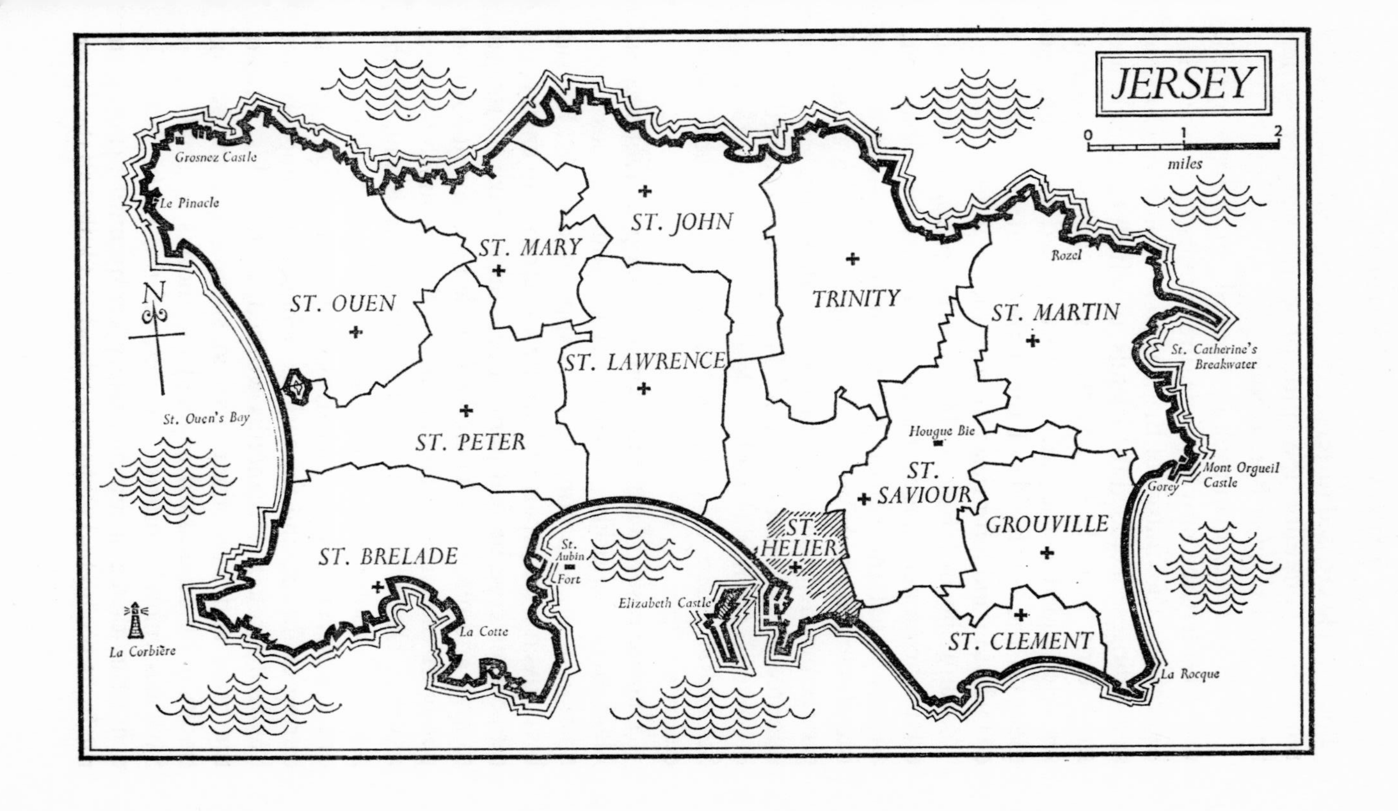
JERSEY
0
1
2
miles
Grosnez Castle
Le Pinacle
N
St. Ouen's Bay
La Corbière
ST. OUEN
ST. MARY
ST. JOHN
TRINITY
ST. MARTIN
Rozel
St. Catherine's Breakwater
Mont Orgueil Castle
Gorey
ST. LAWRENCE
ST. PETER
Hougue Bie
ST. SAVIOUR
GROUVILLE
ST. HELIER
ST. BRELADE
St. Aubin
Fort
Elizabeth Castle
La Cotte
ST. CLEMENT
La Rocque

Marcouf. He crossed to Jersey in A.D. 540, and established a religious community, the spirit of which was kept going later by the Priory of Bonne Nuit.

Then a greater man took up the task, St. Sampson; he it was who left the moving signature 'Sampson a sinner'. He had risen in the Church of Brittany to be Bishop of Dol, and as the diocese included the islands, of which he already had some knowledge, he led a missionary expedition to Guernsey. He landed at the harbour since named after him, and there on the south side of the harbour entrance he had a chapel built and left priests to carry on the work.

Meanwhile, in Jersey, St. Helier, a disciple of St. Marcouf, established a hermitage on a rock near the present harbour, and extended the Christian mission to the south of the island. He did not have very long for this task, as a band of pirates invaded the island in 559 and slew him. About six hundred years later a Guillaume Hamon, who claimed to be descended from the raiders' leader, built the Abbey of St. Helier there in expiation of this killing and richly endowed it.

The successor of St. Sampson as Bishop of Dol was St. Magloire (Maglorius), a Briton from South Wales and a relation of St. Sampson, who was appointed in 565. He had been given a large part of Sark by an Armorican chief for a miraculous cure he had performed, and to Sark he retired to pray and meditate. There he founded a convent to train young missionaries to go out among the pagans in the area around. This was sited in the north of the island, in the place still known as La Moinerie. The rule of St. Magloire's order was very severe—six strokes of the lash for a cough during chanting, and for serious offences anything up to a hundred strokes. His monks worked in the fields, tended the bees, and lived their lives in silence, but the strong tradition he established enabled the monks to hold on in Sark for many centuries, in spite of the raids. There is definite evidence of this monastery lasting until 1412, when the French who had raided the island and killed all the other inhabitants allowed them to leave for France. St. Magloire's miraculous healing powers also bore fruit in Guernsey: there a chieftain Nivo who held part of the island asked him over to cure his dumb daughter, and Magloire's reward this time was land in the Vale parish. He founded a chapel, and fields still bear his name to this day.

These four heroic saints, St. Sampson, St. Marcouf, St. Helier, and St. Magloire, bore the brunt of the missionary work among the islanders, and started the process by which the Islands were linked with progressive civilizing influences beginning to be felt in North-west France. But these priests were members of the Celtic Church. This was a much more mystical and loosely knit organization than the Roman Church; the bishops were travelling evangelists rather than church lords tied to an area, whose dogma and practices, such as the date of Easter, had considerable differences from the Roman. So the Islands for some two hundred years went their own way more or less as Christian communities, incorporating in their festivals many of the old pagan rites with a Christian twist to them, and as was only common sense founding their little chapels at places which were already hallowed by centuries' old tradition as holy to some spirit or god.

There are memories of this process in the story of St. Sampson, who when he visited Jersey gave medals to the children on condition that they stayed away from the festival at Christmas when the pagans worshipped the sun in their rites and disguised themselves as animals. Another ancient custom connected with the end of the year was the practice of wrapping up a log of wood in fantastic clothes, and after a procession burning it at *le vieux bout de l'an.* In Puritan times this practice was condemned by the Royal Court, but it managed to survive, being cunningly transferred to Guy Fawkes Day. Even now the Guy is known as a *Boudelau.* Another example of the pagan practice of fire or sun worship, on which the early missionaries and the Puritans later equally frowned, was the celebration in Alderney of the first Sunday in Lent, or the Dimanche de Brandons, when young men and girls put on masks and danced round and even through a bonfire. In Guernsey, on Midsummer Eve, fires were lit on a big flat-topped rock, Roque Balan, with dancing, and orgies no doubt.

A glimpse of the struggle which went on between the old faiths and the new religion comes from a legend about one of the Pea Stack rocks in Guernsey, called L'Bouan Homme Andriou. An Drio recalls Arch Druid, and the tale is that the great Saint Patrick and his disciples enchanted the Arch Druid and his followers, and confined them to the places which bear their names. It was to this rock that a Jersey-man was later reputed to have tied a hawser and tried to tow away the island, shouting out, 'Hale Pierre, Hale Jean. Guernesi s'en vient.' Luckily the rope broke.

Another phase in the struggle is recalled by the name La chaire de St. Bonit given to a flat stone at the foot of a ten-foot obelisk in the Hamelins district in Guernsey. St. Bonit was Bishop of Auvergne towards the end of the seventh century, a great missionary and traveller, and he possibly visited the island and sat and preached to the people from this old Druid's stone.

During these centuries there was at least one Roman Catholic visitor. In 577 the unfortunate Archbishop of Rouen, Praetextatus, was banished to Jersey for getting involved in a conspiracy to dethrone the Frankish king, and as he lived in exile there for seven years, he may have had some success against the, to him, heretical views of the Celtic churchmen on such things as Easter, the tonsure and the role of women in the services.

At last, at the end of the eighth century, Charlemagne sent the Abbot of Fontenelle to bring the Islands under the jurisdiction of the see of Coutances, at that time in Neustria. But it is tempting to trace back to those early influences the seeds of Nonconformity which have flourished in the Islands at one period or another ever since.

Apart from this sketchy religious and ecclesiastical history there is little evidence for these centuries, often called the Dark Ages in English history books. One can only guess that the little farming settlements on the best plots of arable land in the Islands went on their laborious way, eking out a livelihood with some coastal fishing as they learnt the techniques of better boatbuilding, and evading if they could the raiders and pirates who swarmed in the Channel in those times.

But one record from Geoffrey of Monmouth tells that *circa* 630 Cadwalla, Prince of North Wales, fled to Ireland after his defeat by Edwin the Saxon at Widdington near Morpeth; there, uncertain and friendless, he was in despair. At last he had the idea of taking refuge with Salomon, king of the Armorican Britons. As he was steering towards Armorica, a great storm arose and the Prince's ship was driven to Garnareia, where he landed with great difficulty. In his sorrow the Prince ate nothing for three days, but on the fourth he was filled with a great desire for venison, and sent his nephew Brian out to shoot a deer. Brian went all over the island, but could find no quarry, no wild beast, so he cut a steak from his own thigh, roasted it and served it to the Prince. This meat helped the Prince to recover, and he sailed on to Armorica, where he was re-equipped to return to Wales and fight the Anglo-Saxons in many more battles.

A hoard of coins dug up in Sark, which were from a mint in south-west France of about A.D. 500, shows that one band at least of Visigoth soldiers, under a raiding chief, put ashore there.

A further clue to the type of raider comes from the modern names of the Islands. In the Antonine Itinerary, a guide-book and book of instruction for Roman officials, there are the Roman names for islands in the Channel area, lying between the Isle of Wight and Ushant. Most scholars agree that Alderney was Ridunia, Jersey Angia, and Guernsey Lesia; this leaves Sarnia, or Sarmia, and Caesarea, the names popularly given to the two big islands, to be reallotted. One can reasonably reckon that Sarnia is Sark, but

Caesarea is unknown. The modern names, Jersey and Guernsey, are more probably Scandinavian than Celtic in origin, 'ey' being the Norse for island. So that it is both interesting and revealing to speculate who was the Norse pirate-farmer called Geirr who gave his name to Jersey, or who was the other one called Wern who gave his name to Guernsey. Another intriguing example of this Norse name influence is the name often connected with megaliths, Pouquelaie, reasonably derived from the Norse for 'goblin-path'; one can imagine from this the superstitious dread with which the tough sea rovers gave this name to the grim granite-lined passages which lead into the burial mounds.

The chronicler of the Norman Abbey of Fontenelle tells of another kind of disaster which fell upon the islanders in 709, when a violent earthquake with tidal waves affected the west of Guernsey. It flooded Vazon Bay where remains of a great forest are visible at low tides to this day and left the rocks, on which the Hanois lighthouse now stands, isolated instead of forming as previously a long peninsula out from the island. This great disturbance had a similar effect on the other side of the Bay of Avranches, where it left Mont St. Michel, previously standing in a marshy forest, among the quicksands where it stands today. Indeed the records of the abbey show that revenues were received from lands all round the coast, which were gradually being submerged, right into the fourteenth century. Another interesting piece of evidence of this is the charter granted by King John to the inhabitants of the Ecrehos Islands and their new owner, the Abbaye de Val Richer. He was ordered to build a chapel on the Ecrehos, as it was by then too dangerous for the islanders to get across to the Cotentin for mass.

Certain it is that Viking raids increased in intensity as the ninth century ended. Chroniclers say that the Cotentin was practically a desert, and the Islands must have been partially depopulated, with their wooden chapels and halls burnt, their huts destroyed, and the survivors, with their families and some livestock, living precariously behind the earthen

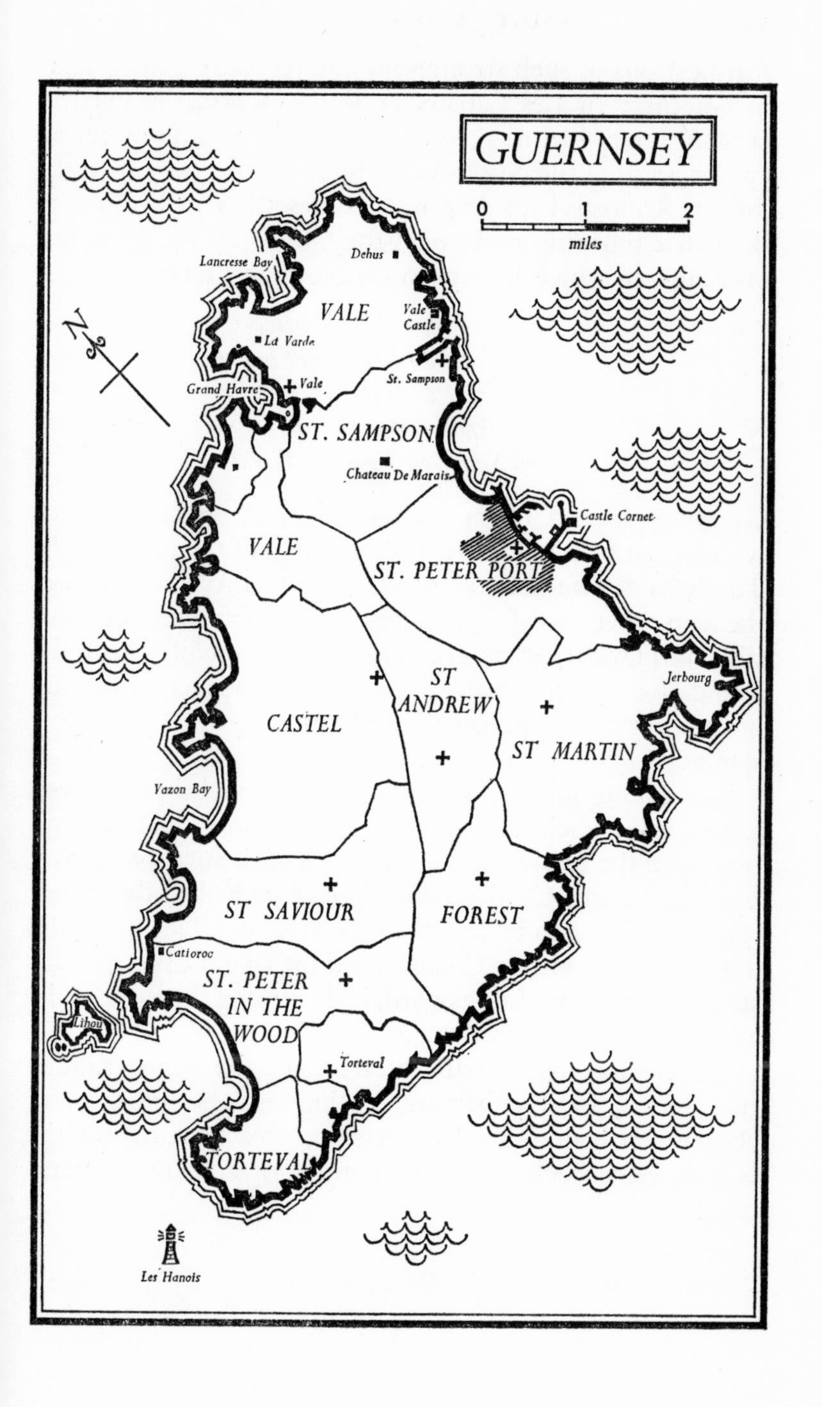
GUERNSEY
0
1
2
miles
N
Lancresse Bay
Dehus
VALE
Vale Castle
La Varde
St. Sampson
Grand Havre
Vale
ST. SAMPSON
Chateau De Marais
Castle Cornet
VALE
ST. PETER PORT
Jerbourg
ST ANDREW
CASTEL
ST MARTIN
Vazon Bay
ST SAVIOUR
FOREST
Catioroc
ST. PETER IN THE WOOD
Lihou
Torteval
TORTEVAL
Les Hanois

fortifications of such strongpoints as Jerbourg promontory in Guernsey or Les Catiaux in Jersey. Wace, the twelfth-century Jersey historian, who was commissioned to write an epic account of the Norse wanderings and the history of the mighty Rollo and his descendants, describes in his Roman de Rou a pillaging raid on all the Islands by the great Jarl Hastings, in which he says in his Norman French:

De sa gent e de sa contree
en plusieurs lieux part le ruine
ke firent la gent Sarrazine
en Aureni, en Guernesi,
en Sairc, en Erm, en Gersi.

Guernsey legend offers another clue. A great cromlech which used to stand in the Vale parish had the name of the Tombeau de Grand Sarrazin or Grand Geffroi. Sarrazin was the name given to all sea-raiders, and Geffroi was very possibly Jarl Godefroy, son of Harold. He is credited with the foundation of the castle, Le Castel, on the commanding position where the parish church of St. Marie du Castro now stands.

The Viking raiders, who had become much bolder, even sailing up the Seine and besieging Paris, won final recognition from the Franks by the Treaty of Clair sur Epte in 911, by which King Charles handed over to Rollo, the Norse leader, the land to be known as Normandy. This grant did not at first include the Cotentin and the Islands, but after his successor, William Longsword, had defeated the Bretons, he added this area to his domain.

During the five hundred years since the vague Roman rule ended, local chieftains, Viking raiders and forceful churchmen had claimed ownership; now in A.D. 933 the Islands came back under the control of a strong government.

Chapter 3

The Duchy of Normandy

AFTER A.D. 933 the Islands were to enjoy a three-hundred-year period of comparative tranquillity, forming as they did an outlying portion of the Duchy of Normandy. The Government was based on Rouen, and at the head was a succession of tough and able dukes, who organized their 'estate' in a thoroughly workmanlike and efficient way. It is probable that only one of them, Robert I, known as Le Diable, the Conqueror's father, actually set foot in the Islands, around the year 1030. The chroniclers state that he had planned a raid on England from Normandy to support Edgar Atheling against Canute. But a great storm off the Sussex coast drove him back and he was driven to the island of 'Gersui, close to the Cotentin'. After he had waited in vain for a change of wind, he then turned his ships to Mont St. Michel and disembarked his host.

Guernsey legend connects this landfall with the island and with the monks of St. Michael du Valle who entertained him. The predecessors of these monks had left Mont St. Michel about sixty years earlier, either because of misconduct or in a reforming spirit, and had founded a priory on part of the island named Clos du Valle; this area in the north-east was cut off except at low tide from the main island. In return for their hospitality Duke Robert confirmed the monks' tenure of the land and instituted them as a priory. It is known that at this date he made over to the monastery of Mont St. Michel the western half of the island, which had been allotted by his father, Richard, to the

Vicomte of the Bessin, Anschetel. The southern and eastern half had been put under the control of Neel, the Vicomte of the Cotentin.

Robert's name is also linked with the bridge, Le Pont de Diable, which he is supposed to have built across the inlet between St. Sampson's and the Vale in Guernsey, and near which he strengthened the defences of the Vale Castle, as a refuge for the rather isolated inhabitants of that area. The Norman ship-master, Restald, who served him at this time, also won a reward, the grant of the little island of Jethou, off Herm.

His allocation of the land to the monastery did not last long, for the new duke, the young William the Bastard, known in English history as the Conqueror, needed the support of the powerful western vicomtes. He re-allotted the western Guernsey Fief to the Vicomte of the Bessin, and later bought the support of the warlike Bishop of Coutances by transferring to his see the island of Alderney, part of the compensation he had given to the Monastery of Mont St. Michel.

Alderney remained divided between the Duke or King and the Bishop for three centuries, the King getting his dues from the windmill, the Bishop from the water-mill, while the little community went on its daily round. They grew wheat on the Blaye, the rich plateau of arable land in the centre and west of the island, which they cultivated on the strip system, a method which has been carried on right down to modern times. On the rest of the island they grazed sheep. No doubt, as in the other islands, this simple farming was supplemented by fishing, and by piracy when a chance occurred.

The Monastery of Mont St. Michel, though it suffered a severe loss of lands and had to wait until the reign of Henry II to regain its fief of a quarter of the island, yet retained its share of the patronage of the ten Guernsey parishes, and received some compensation in a rather barren tract, Noirmont, in Jersey, and in the island of Sark. Later

Sark passed to the powerful de Vernon family, who had connections with Pierre de Préaulx, the Lord of the Channel Isles at the end of the Norman period.

In accordance with the pattern, the other small island, Herm, was used to endow a monastic house. Duke William gave it to the Augustinians of Cherbourg, who developed there a flourishing religious community. The Prior became a man of importance, who claimed to hold a Court of Assize, with judgment over life and limb, and he had the right of wreckage, over whatever useful or valuable flotsam was washed up from the swirling seas. The little monastery developed farming, and stocked the island with sheep and cattle. As so often happens in a medieval monastery, there was a carp-pond, which was later to be the private possession of the Governors of Guernsey.

Incidentally it was the monks of the Islands who were credited with the introduction of the cattle from France, cattle of the Isigny breed and the breed called Froment de Leon, from which the Islands' distinctive strains of cattle are descended.

In a similar way to the original allocation of the good arable areas in Guernsey, areas already farmed for centuries, to form the basis of the two great fiefs, the Bessin and the Cotentin, important Norman families received additional holdings in Jersey. For example, the de Carterets in the area of St. Ouen's, and the families of de Sottevaast, de Vainville, and de Barneville. These fiefs might pass to ecclesiastical tenants, or might be subdivided into sub-fiefs held by Norman knights. Yet they all owed the Duke services and dues, as the basic principle of feudalism laid down. For he was the super-landlord. These tenants were known as franc or free tenants, or were given the name 'suitors', as one of their main obligations was attendance at the Duke's court. None of these fiefs was large enough on its own to call for knight service, so that their other duties were of two kinds—one of which was the mundane one of a tax, or relief, when it was called for. This was paid in livre tournois (i.e. of Tours), a currency which has been used for centuries in the Islands as a just and convenient means of estimating value, since so often the franc or sterling fluctuated widely, and still today the livre tournois is used in property documents.

The other dues to the Duke were a strange assortment of services. The Seigneur of Rozel had to ride into the sea up to the girths of his horse to meet the Duke if he should come come to Jersey. In Guernsey the Seigneur of the Fief les Eperons owed a pair of spurs; this due was paid in 1957 by the holder of the fief when Queen Elizabeth II visited the island. An unpopular service was that exacted from the Seigneur d'Anneville who had to keep under strict guard any prisoner of the King who had been convicted of a minor offence.

The franc tenants, the seigneurs of the islands, with their manors and their domain land, claimed of course dues and services from their tenants. These included attendance at the Fief Court, where the seigneur had the right of minor justice over any of his vassals found guilty in his court; there he would deal with all cases of money or goods due to him, with quarrels between tenants, and other matters needing attention from the master of the lands. In this Court he was aided and advised by his officials, the Sénéschal, the Vavasseurs, the Greffier, the Prévôt, and the Sargent. Even today the Feudal Court of some of the fiefs still survives, meeting in the open or in a special little courthouse, and there the officials gather, but only to collect certain dues.

The seigneur also exacted certain services on his own farm lands from his tenants. They were expected to help cart his grain, and to clean out his barns and his pigeon-cote, the Colombier, the right to which was a valuable seigneurial privilege and an addition to the winter's meat supply. They had to take the conger eels they caught all round the coasts to be dried at the special place the lord provided; it was known as an eperquerie, from the sticks which held open the split conger to be dried over a furze fire before they were exported to be eaten in Normandy and England on the many fish days of the Roman Church. The tenants had to pay for this service, as they had to pay the Duke for the final process before export; they had to take the dried fish to the Salerie, the salting point, and there the curing was completed. Later in the days of Edward I when official control had evolved into the duty to sell the catch, caught between Easter and Michaelmas, to the King, the fishermen won a charter, by which they were permitted to fish for mackerel, herring and other lesser kinds, in return for a money payment.

On one or two fiefs the tenants had the obligation to defend their seigneur in battle, and to carry him by boat to the four ports of Normandy once in his lifetime or in theirs. But for most the remaining obligation was a money payment. In Jersey, by the Middle Ages, these payments had been consolidated in one aid, at the rate of so many sols per bouvée, a bouvée being the equivalent of five acres.

But in Guernsey different payments survived. The most important was champart, a tithe payment on the corn and flax crop. Other dues with intriguing names were poulage, a due of two hens for every inhabited house, a due for which certain householders are liable to this day; fouage, a hearth tax; pesnage on the acorns eaten by pigs in the manor woods, and werp, the delightful name for the due on the beasts who strayed onto the manor pasturages. Today there are fines for animals found straying, without being properly tethered, on the common lands. But the islanders' practice of tethering their cows in lines in the pastures arises from the shortage of pasture and the richness of the grass, not from fear of werp.

The Duke had his humbler tenants too. They owed him similar dues and services for the small farms, or bordages, which, divided into long strips called caruées, they cultivated with a shallow plough drawn by oxen. These the tenants of the area provided on a co-operative basis. These bordiers, yeomen or peasant farmers, played a very important part in the island communities, and were on quite a different footing from the humble people on the bottom of the feudal ladder in England.

There was no serfdom in the Islands. Apart from the comparatively trivial labour services mentioned above and the payments in money or kind they had to hand over, the bordiers were free to get on with their own daily labours on their farms. They were people of importance in their locality, able to inherit their lands, and responsible for 'good order' among the people of their area. One, no doubt, unpopular duty was to provide an escort for prisoners from prison to their trial, and, if convicted, on from there to the field where the gibbet stood.

This situation probably dates back to the earliest period of Norman rule. For the Islands had been badly depopulated by the sea raiders, and the Dukes could only get farming families to come over from the mainland to fill up the gaps where farms were destroyed and lands desolated by offering them this very reasonable contract. Of course there was bound to be a demand for labour on the seigneurs' lands, the abbeys' lands and the fields of the richer bordiers, but this was found from the hired labour of the poorer peasants.

This memory of the ancient laws and customs of the Islands, 'customs used in the Islands time out of mind', which neither the Duke nor the seigneurs nor later the centralizing English Government was able to break down, has been a vital force in the islanders' story. By it, for instance, the islanders claimed the inalienable right not to have to undergo any military service, with the interesting exception that 'they will go with the Duke of Normandy, if need be, when he goes in person to recover England.' Another right to which they held fast was that of not being tried for any cause in a court outside the island nor by any law except their own.

The Duke, as supreme seigneur, had some overall rights, which were only parted with sparingly to a favoured franc tenant. The mills were his, and the tenants had to bring their corn and oats to be ground there, and to carry timber for the repair of the mills; even today an area in Guernsey, where the States Water Board has its waterworks, is named the King's Mills.

He had the right to the 'princely things', the 'great fish' and the 'royal birds'. He had his rights of warren, the chasing of rabbits, which were the only game. But these rights varied in the Islands. In Jersey where the ducal estates were scattered throughout the island, he had warrens like the other seigneurs. In Guernsey, where his main area of land was in the south-east, he treated the whole island as a warren, except for one or two privileged enclosures. One of these was the warren, or garenne, about one hundred yards square and surrounded by a moat, which was the possession of the Seigneur d'Anneville, at one time a de Chesney, a relative of the d'Albini family and so descendant of the original Vicomtes de St. Sauveur, who had owned the north-west half of Guernsey as early as 1020. This family claimed the hereditary right 'from time immemorial' to chase conies with a dog and staff without other engine from September to February. Throughout the west of the island the Duke had precedence, to go out with dogs, sticks, ferrets and nets, and after him might come the Abbot of Mont St. Michel, the Seigneur of Fief le Comte, and other franc tenants. One wonders how often the Abbot crossed the stormy and treacherous waters of the Bay of Avranches to chase a rabbit.

The Duke granted some of the wastelands—the high scrubland, called Les Landes, the sandy soil called Les Mielles, the heavy wet marshlands called Les Marais—to tenants, notably the abbeys, as they were land improvers. But he kept control of a large area himself. On one part, in Guernsey, near Castel Church, he had the right to hold a market, so that this area is still known as Les Landes du Marché. It is possible that this particular site was chosen as being a convenient meeting place between the peasant farmers of the south of the island and the fishermen from the inlets in the north. At any rate one can presume that St.

Peter Port was too exposed to attack from the sea, too difficult of access from the farming areas and too insignificant at this time to justify the honour of a market.

Another valuable right which he parted with sparingly was the right to sea wreck, to all the objects and articles washed up on the shores of the Islands by the dangerous and destructive seas. This right was all-embracing in Jersey, Sark, Herm and Alderney; but in Guernsey where the north-west coast was by far the most fruitful area, he shared it with the Abbot and the Seigneur of Le Comte.

From this period date two interesting customs, one of which lasted until 1837, and the second is still legal. One of the duties of the feudal court of the Abbey of St. Michael was the inspection of the local sea defences and the highways. From this developed the custom of the Chevauchée, by which the officers of this court, sénéschal and vavasseurs, and the officers of the island, the Sheriff, the Serjeant, Greffier, Comptroller, Procureur, Receiver, and the important officer called the Porte-Lance went on a tour of the roads and parishes. The Porte-Lance carried a wand of eleven and a quarter feet which must not meet any obstruction on the road, and so they went their way inspecting and stopping at intervals for refreshments. They were accompanied by footmen, Les Pions, who had the privilege of kissing every woman they met with on the road. There can still be seen, near Pleinmont Point, Guernsey, a flat and grassy mound with an encircling ring of stones, the Table des Pions, where these footmen were served with refreshment at this remote spot on their route; their superiors, the Cavaliers, did their eating and drinking by the Château de Pezeries just down the road.

The other ancient and curious custom is the Clameur de Haro. By this procedure, if an islander considers his estate to be injured or his rights infringed, he may kneel on the ground at the spot, in the presence of two witnesses, and cry out: 'Haro, Haro, à l'aide, mon Prince. On me fair tort.'

If he is in Guernsey, he must complete the cry with the

Lord's Prayer in French. This acts as an injunction, and the case has to be lodged with the Royal Court and tried there. Many times down the centuries has this procedure been used. One of the most notable occasions was in 1850, when one of the Tupper family thus saved the ancient fortifications of Castle Cornet from being demolished. As recently as 1956 a Madame Picot in Alderney used the Clameur to stop building operations.

By all these arrangements the Norman dukes organized the legal, social and economic life of the Islands; they allotted the lands; the dues and services were established and recognized, ducal and seigneurial courts were set up to enforce them, and itinerant justices were sent over periodically from Rouen to see that the machinery was working smoothly. But there were two elements which may date from pre-Norman times.

The first was the office of Jurat, about the origin of which historical experts disagree. In the important document of 1248 'Les franchises que le roi d'engleterre a en Guernesi et que les hommes de Guernesi ont', the office of Jurat is definitely traced back to John's reign. But it is very reasonable to suppose that he was adapting an older institution, similar to the hommes jugeurs of Normandy, that is a bench of men of local standing (optimates patrie) chosen as judgment-finders, before whom the islanders had a guarantee that their cases would be tried according to local customs.

Quite possibly this safeguard was one of the considerations for which the native islanders and the Norman peasant settlers agreed to pay their rentes, or land-dues, to the Duke. It also seems quite possible that these Jurats were originally the parish headmen, chosen by each parish in open meeting at the church door; as a body these men would represent the views and claims of the island communities. Certainly the Jurats, whose presence and participation in the proceedings of the Royal Courts were essential, are a vital element in the evolving constitutions of the Islands, and their numbers, twelve in Jersey, twelve in Guernsey, seven in Alderney, and six in Sark, correspond closely, at any rate in the larger islands, to the number of parishes.

The second pre-Norman element was the parish. There was an ancient ceremony called une ouie de paroisse—'in the hearing of the parish'—by which all legal acts of importance took place in the parish church, officially in the presence of the whole parish community. Even agreements made in the Royal Court were subsequently confirmed in this way. This seems good evidence that the parishes had developed an identity, even perhaps some form of parish assembly with officers, in pre-Norman times.

This useful local organization was then carried on under the regime of the Norman Dukes, even though there was the rival organization of the manor courts. Certainly by the fourteenth century the parish provided a jury of presentment or witness for the visits of the justices. Information collected parish by parish was the basis of the extentes or inquiries which were held into the extent of the King's rights or island customs; and the parish was made into a police unit, whose duty it was to pursue malefactors, keep watch at night, see that a suspect who sought sanctuary did not escape from church, and even to keep a prisoner in custody.

The parishes obviously centred on the churches, and it is to the early eleventh century that most of the fine little granite churches date, though, owing to the impossibility of shaping granite beyond a few simple mouldings, there is little in the style of the actual buildings to give a clue. There were clearly churches of some sort before this time; indeed in the Vale church a big stone marked with a cross and Alpha and Omega, and dated to the seventh century, has been found. But they probably went up in flames in the wild tenth century, and their sites offered an opportunity and a challenge to the Normans, devout Christians and keen builders, to build again in granite the twelve parish churches in Jersey and the ten in Guernsey.

St. Mary's and St. Martin's in Jersey are mentioned in a

charter of April 1042, and St. Peter Port, ecclesia Sancti Petri de Portu, is assigned in a deed of Duke William to the great Benedictine Abbey of Marmoutiers in 1048. This Abbot and the Abbot of Mont St. Michel were the patrons for much of the Middle Ages of many of the Islands' churches; but for general ecclesiastical supervision each island had its Dean, and the parishes came under the Bishop of Coutances, a sensible arrangement while the Duchy of Normandy lasted intact, but one to cause great complications later on.

Not that the building of some of the churches was a simple process, according to legend. One, St. Martin, Guernsey, was planned to be built on a corner of ground near Saint's Bay, but when the building was started all the materials and tools were moved by unknown hands to the present site, and the original site, known as the Coin de la Biche, Corner of the Nanny Goat, for long had a sombre reputation. Even as late as the 1800's a cottager of this district, returning with a cartload of vraic (seaweed), was stopped at this corner by a great hairy grey nanny-goat, the spectre which haunted the spot.

But there were other happier beliefs. Widespread was the faith in the power of the water of Holy Wells, to cure such illnesses as rheumatism, erysipelas, inflammation of the eyes, illnesses summarized as Mal de la Fontaine. One of the most famous of these was the well of St. George. It was linked in legend with Egregoire, the Watcher, L'ange qui veille, who mounted the white horse which led to victory.

An old tale of this well illustrates early inter-island rivalry. St. Patrick had left Jersey, where the Jerseymen, Crapauds, had treated him very rudely and pelted him with stones, and he had arrived in Guernsey where he was given a great welcome. St. George, too, happened to be in the island, and the two saints met at this well. After a quarrel as to which saint the island should belong in future, they remembered their saintliness, and decided it would be better for both to give the island a blessing and then to depart.

So St. Patrick filled his wallet with many noxious things, such as snakes and toads, clearing Guernsey of them, and returned to Jersey where he emptied his wallet. St. George gave his blessing and the power to cure disease and childlessness to the stream of water from the well.

The well had its own chapel hard by. This chapel was certainly in existence in 1156, and was built on a site which had been holy from prehistoric times; a very sacred and important place. There was held the Fief Court of Le Comte, whose seal had the symbolic figure of St. George upon it.

A delightful tale, which has possible traces of historical fact embedded in it, is told to this day to explain the small stature of the island people.

Long ago there lived near Vazon a very beautiful girl, who went each day to the meadow to milk her cows. One day she found there lying asleep a very handsome young man dressed in grass-green, with his bow and arrows by his side. He was very small. As she stared he awoke, told her he was a fairy and offered her his hand. She accepted and they went off to the seashore and sailed away. Many, many years later, when the girl was almost forgotten, a man noticed a host of little men swarming out of an ancient dolmen, the Creux ès Fées, and asked them who they were. The leader told him that they had been delighted by the beauty of the girl one of them had married and they had come to collect wives. He ordered the mortal to tell the islanders to hand over their wives and daughters. Naturally the islanders refused, and then a running battle followed in which the island men were defeated and slain. The little men took over the island, and its women, for a number of years, but at last their laws compelled them to re-embark and sail away. But after that many families were of small stature, and no Guernsey witch needed a broomstick to fly through the air to her meeting-place.

In spite of, or perhaps because of this fairy influence, the pattern of island life developed under the Norman dukes, little affected by the ups and down in neighbouring lands. It is not known if any islanders accompanied their Duke when he sailed for Hastings and the conquest of England. There may have been some island seamen with the fleet, and some of the names are similar, des Préauex, du Cherne, de la Landes, de Carterey. But the Duke's uncle, Archbishop Mauger of Rouen, was definitely banished to Guernsey for having dared to excommunicate his powerful nephew. Traditionally he landed at Saint's Bay, near which he lived during his stay and practised magic with a familiar spirit named Thoret. He also had several children by a local girl named Gille. The Guilles and the Maugers have been well-known local families for generations. One of his 'descendants' married Richard Cromwell, son of the Protector, and another was rewarded by Henry V with a seigneurie for his gallant action in 1419, when this Jaques Mauger brought a force of islanders to the mouth of the River Agon and stormed and captured the fortress of Mont Marin near Coutances.

After the death of William the Conqueror, Normandy passed to his eldest son Robert, and England passed to William Rufus, while the third son Henry had to be content for the moment with five thousand marks of silver. But, luckily for the Islands, control of the Cotentin was sold by Robert to Henry, and so they shared in his strong, fair government at a time when the other sections of the Norman Empire were in a chronic state of unrest. Then after the death of Rufus and the collapse of Robert's cause they found themselves reunited with the other territories under Henry's rule.

Naturally enough in the struggle for power between Stephen Count of Blois and Geoffrey Plantagenet, fighting to secure the rights of his son Henry, the islanders stuck loyally by their overlord, Henry Duke of Normandy, and were rewarded when Geoffrey, who swallowed Normandy bit by bit 'as if it were an artichoke', regained the Cotentin and islands in the campaign of 1142. He confirmed their rights and their customs.

Their royal overlord was also more directly concerned with their prosperity from now on, as two great fief-holders, Roger of the Cotentin and Ranulph Earl of Chester, were partisans of Stephen and so forfeited their estates. Some of this land was kept in the King's hands, so increasing the Fief le Roi in Guernsey, and on this land as well as on the lands of Le Comte and St. Michael the land tax was to be paid to the Ducal Exchequer. In Jersey similarly—where the island was divided into three districts, de Gorroic, de Groceio, and de Crapout Doit—the Duke's taxes were collected throughout the island. For the privilege of collecting these three local Jersey landowners paid the Duke a total of £440.

This increase in the ducal holdings in the Islands had an important effect on the organization of their government. Up to the year 1177 the two islands had been administered together by the Sénéschal of Normandy, who appointed a deputy to represent his interests and power in the Islands. Already before this date there was a Royal Court in Guernsey, which had its own seal and was presided over by a Vicomte. Now, because of the increase of business, this court gained in importance, and the two islands were administered separately under two deputies.

When Richard I became King and Duke in 1189, his brother John was created Count of Mortain, and about 1195 he was given the Lordship of the Isles. Though this grant probably did not include Sark, Alderney and the smaller islands, it meant that he was responsible for the safety and government of the Islands, and the revenues from them went to his purse. On his accession to the English throne in 1199 John, who knew that the Cotentin nobles were some of his most troublesome subjects, wished to separate the control of the Islands from Normandy, and so he rewarded one of his loyal Norman supporters, Pierre de Préauex, with the same lordship.

So it was to this Norman noble that the islanders were supposed to look for guidance and leadership in the troubled years from 1200. What would be their fate as John struggled by fits and starts to keep together his Angevin inheritance, the kingdom of England and the French states of Normandy, Anjou, Brittany and Aquitaine, against the counter-claims of Arthur and the shrewd intervention of Phillipe Auguste of France?

Chapter 4

The Growth of Nationhood

To keep control of Normandy against the cunning and ruthless pressure of Philippe Auguste called for strong rule and good leadership. Henry II had given the Normans strong rule, and Richard had been an inspiring leader. John was neither strong nor inspiring. The years before his accession had been ones of invasion, alarms, and very heavy taxation, and the Normans now began to wonder if the price of this connection was worth paying.

Although John at the start had the best of the struggle to keep his inheritance, he soon threw away his advantages. By his foolish divorce of his childless wife and marriage to another Isabella, he stirred up many enemies, from England to Aquitaine. He then alienated many more supporters by his brutal treatment of noble captives, and finally he ruined his cause by the murder of Arthur of Brittany. His cause was hopeless, and on 6th December 1203 he abandoned his continental possessions and landed in England. 'Let be, let be. One day I shall win it all again,' he is reported to have said.

His writ now ran only in Gascony and part of Poitou, where the great towns of Bordeaux and Bayonne stood loyal, and in the Channel Islands.

Yet in the Islands there was desperate confusion. Pierre de Préaulx, after holding out desperately in Rouen, had finally abandoned hope of help from John and had surrendered that key city: this action led to Préaulx forfeiting his Lordship of the Islands. Many of the Norman nobles, who held lands in the Islands, fought or intrigued on the French side

1 La Gran' mère du Chimquière, St. Martin's, Guernsey

2 St. Ouen's Manor, Jersey (*by permission of G. Malet de Carteret and S. Senett Esq.*)

and John was so uncertain that in 1204 he sent a mercenary commander, Eustace le Moine, a renegade monk turned pirate whom he employed, to harry and destroy the Islands. Although De Carteret of St. Ouen's, Jersey, tried to organize a local defence, 'nought was left to burn'.

However by 1207 the Islands were brought securely under the King's control, and De Suligny was sent as Governor, with a strong force to support him.

De Suligny had to deal with a difficult situation. A number of the greater landowners were Norman nobles fighting on the French side, and much of the lands in all the Islands were the possessions of Abbeys and Priories in France. At the same time the islanders had strong links, of government, customs, trade and in spiritual matters, with Normandy, and were very jealous of their privileges. A mixture of force and conciliation solved the problem. The estates of 'Norman' lords, those with pro-French sympathies, were confiscated, and hostages were taken even from those who appeared to be loyal.

But John made no alterations in the Norman law to which the islanders were accustomed, and he confirmed their traditional customs, those rights 'from time immemorial' which were the cornerstone of their liberties. He also very soon restored the rights and possessions of the Norman Abbeys and of the Bishop of Coutances, which were the framework of the Islands' ecclesiastical establishment. He knew that from the keep of Gorey Castle one can see the spire of Coutances Cathedral, and that, as one anxious warden observed, 'One may twice in a day cross the sea between us and them.'

An attempt was made to check the economic links between the Islands and Normandy by barring the export of fish, the Islands' main commodity, to Normandy. But one may doubt how effective this ruling was, as later, in the French wars, on many occasions islanders trading in Normandy are reported to have been cut off by the outbreak of hostilities.

The most important task was to create a form of government to replace the Islands' dependence on centralized rule from Rouen. This was done by the appointment by the King, as Duke of Normandy, of a warden as his personal representative to rule the Islands. The warden was directly responsible to him for their government. He had to defend them, to collect and administer the 'Duke's' revenues, to hold the 'ducal' courts in the King's name, and to hold the Assizes at the customary times. In doing all this the warden held a very important place as a royal official, similar in responsibility to the Sénéschal of Gascony.

For the Islands were now in a key position, for two reasons. As ships then with their meagre navigational aids worked from headland to headland, the Islands, and the haven of St. Peter Port in particular, were the only safe port of call for ships working their way from English ports down to Gascony and back. If there were storms, or if war flared up between England and France, or if Breton pirates lurked, there only could ships shelter. Secondly, if England and France were at war, a situation which arose many times in the following centuries, the Islands were a base and an outpost, from which a threat of attack could be mounted against the mainland only a comparatively few miles away.

De Suligny's first task then was to defend the Islands and it is he who is credited with the start of the building of the two fine castles. The strongpoint in Jersey was Gorey Castle, which towers up on its impregnable cliff on the eastern point of the island looking out grimly towards the French coast. In Guernsey the building of Castle Cornet had begun by 1206. Though early records are vague, it is clear that it comprised a keep and two courtyards, standing on a boss of rock at the northern end of its little island. This island guarded the haven by which St. Peter Port grew up, protecting it both from enemies and from south-westerly gales, and as it could only be reached from Guernsey proper at low water, it was fairly impregnable. But it had a weakness. If its assailants had command of the sea, then it could be cut off, and it was very difficult for the islanders to reinforce it and to use it as a place of refuge for themselves.

Thus, in Guernsey, the main royal castle was supplemented by other defences. One was the Château de Marais, a fortified refuge on the edge of a marshy area, with a wet ditch surrounding it. A second was Jerbourg Castle, the fortified promontory on the south-east point of the island, which from the 1300's was the responsibility of the de Sausmarez family. The head of the family was hereditary Castellan. In fact, in 1811, the Governor of that time, Sir John Doyle, warned the seigneur, Mr. Matthew de Sausmarez, that he was expected to take command of Jerbourg Castle in the event of invasion.

The defences and garrisons of the Islands were first tested in 1212, when Eustace the Monk sailed to attack them. He had deserted to Philippe Auguste with five of the King's galleys, and swooped down to try to repeat his previous raid. He was repulsed from Jersey and Guernsey, but managed to seize Sark, where he left a force of his freebooting followers.

In the following year King John himself sailed to the Islands, landing in Jersey on the first stage of an obstinate attempt to recover his overseas dominions. He brought only his personal followers with him, for he hoped to shame the unwilling and distrustful barons of England into supporting the venture. But no one followed him and he had to sail angrily back again.

However his presence may have stirred the new warden, Philippe d'Aubigny, into dealing with the pirates on Sark. Certainly in 1214 he attacked the fortress island and sent Eustace the Monk's men as prisoners to Winchester. King John wrote, 'We return you many thanks for your faithful service to vindicate our honour. We also send you back your hostages, because we have full confidence in your fidelity.'

After the collapse of John's continental allies at the Battle of Bouvines, and the rising of the English barons against him, this able warden left the Islands for England to help his king. This gave another opportunity to Eustace the Monk, who sailed to the Islands with his powerful fleet and seized them for the French cause. He was finally brought to account in 1217, when d'Aubigny caught up with him at the naval battle of Sandwich. Eustace the Monk was bringing reinforcements across to support the Lord Louis, the French King's son, in his attempt to win the crown of England, during the confusion which followed John's death and the accession of Henry III. D'Aubigny with his ships intercepted Eustace and beheaded him on his own quarter-deck.

The position of the Islands was cleared up for the time being by the 8th clause of the Treaty of Lambeth, which read, 'Concerning the Isles. The Lord Louis shall send letters to the brethren of Eustace the Monk, ordering them to give them back to the Lord Henry of England, and if they surrender them not, the Lord Louis shall compel them to do so.'

The Islands were then surrendered, but, apart from the damage, this dangerous period brought increased suspicion by the King's officials of the loyalty of the chief landowners. An inquiry was held and more land was confiscated. In fact, in Jersey, of all the important Norman families, the De Carterets seem to have been the only survivors; and it was made a rule that any landowner who spent more than a week in Normandy should have his estates confiscated.

For the next fifty years or so the Islands passed through a comparatively peaceful period—the lull before the storms of the fourteenth century. Until 1254 a succession of wardens were appointed by the King to administer the Islands as a separate parcel of the royal domain. These wardens had to be administrators and soldiers, but the emphasis at this time was on administration. They were generally drawn from men who had proved themselves as sheriffs; constables, forest wardens or royal justices in England, but the names of Gascons are also found among them, for an increasing number of Gascons came to settle in the Islands, owing to their trading links. They controlled much of the wine trade, they leased fisheries, they bought land, and at least one, John de Contes, was Bailiff of Guernsey and later warden of the Islands from 1271 to 1275. One Gascon, Pierre de Garis, bought a Guernsey farm, which is still in the hands of the family today.

These wardens were responsible for collecting the revenue from the Islands and for using the necessary portion of it to cover their expenses; the main expense of course was defence, payment of the garrisons of the castles and the cost of their upkeep, for the warden was also keeper of the castles and captain of the garrisons. From the revenue the warden also deducted his 'salary', and, if it were in the terms of his commission, he was liable to pay so many marks per annum into the Exchequer in London.

Like the sheriff of an English county the warden had to carry out the King's administrative orders. This duty was complicated by the fact that his command was an outpost, that there were close economic and ecclesiastical ties with Normandy, and that he had to humour the Island magnates who insisted on their own 'laws and customs'.

The administration of justice in the King's name was his responsibility too. He had to hold assizes every three years, and he presided, with the Island Jurats, over the 'Royal Courts', to deal with minor cases and with preparatory work before the assizes were held.

The warden was an all-powerful official and must have been a very busy man. Obviously he had assistants, but how they were organized, except that each castle had a constable, is not known.

In 1254 Prince Edward was given the Lordship of the Isles by his father Henry. This meant that he was virtually the Duke, and as such he had the right to all the assets and was responsible for the Islands' administration and defence. But it does not appear that this change had any real effect in the Islands.

The wardens during this period seem to have been able and upright men, who conscientiously guarded and administered their island domain, and resisted pressure from overpowerful subjects. Some of the local magnates were men of importance; for instance Henry III gave the Manor of Anneville in Guernsey to Sir William de Chesney, a kinsman of the warden d'Aubigny. As this de Chesney also bought the large manor of Fief le Comte from Baldwin de Vere, he became one of the most powerful landowners in the Islands, and would expect his views and rights to be considered. His widow found herself involved in a big lawsuit brought by the Abbot of Mont St. Michel who, as the possessor of two large manors in Jersey, about one-quarter of Guernsey and the islands of Lihou, Jethou, and Chausey, had great influence. He asserted his overlordship of the de Chesney estates, and tried to bribe the warden to give him a favourable verdict. But the warden stood firm for the rights of the widow.

The Islands then were fortunate in avoiding the intrigues which distracted England under the weak but high-handed Henry—the evil influence of foreign favourites, Poitevins, Provençals, Savoyards, and Papalists. Nor were they affected by the Civil War which broke out between Henry and Simon de Montfort with his programme of 'constitutional' government.

But with the accession of Edward I the situation was to change. He appointed as warden, and then as Lord of the Isles for life, Otto de Grandison. Otto was a Burgundian knight who had prospered and done well in the King's service, and was promoted to high offices, secretary to the King and Sénéschal of Gascony. It was Otto who was chosen to lead most of the important embassies during Edward's reign. As he was such a prominent and busy man —who in fact never even visited the Islands until he was over ninety years old—the administration had to be organized to function in his absence.

Gradually the warden's duties were divided, with a bailiff in each island exercising his judicial functions, and a subwarden carrying out the other duties. This division had a vital effect on the whole future of the Islands. For Otto de Grandison simply looked on them as an 'estate', the purpose of which was to provide him with the necessary income. He appointed his own men to be the officials, and, if they feathered their own nests at the same time as they gathered in his revenue, he was not concerned. But, owing to the complexities of island law, it came to be the custom that the bailiff was a local man. His position at the head of the Royal Court was strengthened by the possession of the official seal for legal documents. Originally Edward I had sent one seal (*quoddam sigillum nostrum*) for use in both the large islands; but somehow it had disappeared by 1304, and two similar seals, with *three leopards passant*, and inscriptions for the two islands, were then used by the bailiffs of Jersey and Guernsey.

It was then round the bailiffs that the resistance to the corruption and tyranny of Otto's officials tended to gather during the following years. There were a number of inquiries conducted by English officials sent over to investigate complaints; but little was done to remedy the fact that in the eyes of the islanders Otto's men tended to be judge and jury in their own cases.

One bailiff of Guernsey, it is true, Guillaume de St. Remy, who had exasperated the islanders by his extortion, was condemned by an inquiry and, after taking sanctuary, fled the island.

This right of sanctuary was very strictly observed, but the islanders would look on grimly as St. Remy went his way. He would be allowed to remain in church for nine days, being fed by his relatives. Then, as the islanders refused to have their churches cluttered up with criminals, he would have to set out on one of the Sanctuary Tracks, called Perquages, to the coast. A priest would go with him to see that he did not wander, and he would pass little chapels or crosses set up *en route* to recall him to repentance. At last he would reach the coast and embark to sail away into exile.

Another factor in promoting this independent spirit may

have been the increase of small landholders at this period. The big estates were being broken down, subdivided, and the smaller farmers were tending to enclose more land, thus acquiring a bigger stake in the community. A reason for this enclosure was the increasing cultivation of parsnips, a crop which suited the island soils, and which as a new crop was exempt from the old Champart tax on wheat.

In 1295 this growing bitterness was overshadowed temporarily by disaster. A brawl had broken out between English and Norman seamen at Bayonne, and a Norman had been killed. In revenge the Normans attacked an English ship and hanged the sailors and the bodies of dogs from the yard-arm, 'and so they sailed, making no difference between a dog and an Englishman'. Ships from both sides gathered, and off St. Mahé in Brittany the English were victorious. But the Frenchmen appealed to the King, Philip le Bel. It seemed a good cause to him, and he summoned Edward to Paris to answer for it. Terms were agreed, by which Edward should formally surrender Gascony, marry the French King's sister, and then be duly restored to the Duchy. But Philip tried to be too clever. When he had occupied the Gascon strongholds he repudiated the treaty. Edward I was infuriated by this trickery and promptly declared war.

This decision put the Islands in the forefront of the battle-line, and for the emergency Otto's sub-warden, the Prior of Wenlock, was replaced by a soldier, Henry de Cobham. However, in the spring the French fleet arrived to attack and destroy all they could. The raiders failed to take the royal castles, but they caused a great deal of damage, sacking and desecrating the churches, and carrying off the plate. It was reported that the Host was thrown upon the ground and spat upon. Many houses in the towns and in the country-side were burnt to the ground, and the newly built jetty at St. Peter Port was destroyed. Women and girls were torn from sanctuary, and the casualties were put at 1,500 men and women.

In a petition to the King after the disaster it was stated:

'The mills that you had in the isle were burnt together with all our goods.' To repair the damage was a considerable task, and ten years later the King authorized a toll on shipping to repair the Guernsey jetty and help in rebuilding the town. In Jersey, where the first reaction of the Government was to strengthen Gorey Castle, the people were angry that wood they vitally needed was being carried off for that purpose.

This attack seems to have drawn Edward's attention more closely to the Islands. For he ordered the building of La Tour Gand, a fortification to cover the northern approaches of St. Peter Port and in particular the Royal Court House and the Royal Grange, the collecting point for his produce.

He also ordered the setting-up of a full inquiry, or general Eyre. This Court was to inquire into all lands, to take the assizes and all other cases, and to hear the islanders' complaints. The chief justice was the Prior of Wenlock, previously a sub-warden, and a cousin of Otto de Grandison, so it is not surprising that complaints against officials were quickly dismissed. Among the criminal cases was that of Sir Drogo de Barentin, Seigneur of Rozel, Jersey, the charges against whom included rape, seizure of other men's property kidnapping and assault. He got away with a fine of three hundred livre tournois.

Then came a shock for the islanders, as the justices produced a bundle of writs, *Quo Warranto*. Edward I was attempting to extend to the Islands the procedure already current in England, by which all his subjects had to be prepared to explain and prove by what warrant they claimed their rights and privileges. The first attack on privileges seems only to have concerned the Seigneurs of Fiefs, but it caused much resentment and was shelved for the moment.

The attack on what the islanders considered their rights continued in later inquiries in the reign of Edward II; but by now the English lawyers grew bolder, challenging the right of the island communities to elect their Jurats, 'who arrogate to themselves the function of the King's Judges'.

The islanders again answered that they had the right from time immemorial, and were governed by the Law of Normandy, as embodied in Le Grand Coutoumier, 'except that we have certain customs used in this island from time immemorial'.

The justices, and Otto's officials, also came up against the Church in this inquiry of 1309. For the Bishop of Coutances, represented on the ground by the Dean of Jersey, had defied a papal proclamation forbidding him to summon ecclesiastical cases to be heard in Normandy. When the justices ordered the Dean to obey, he excommunicated them, and when they imprisoned him he escaped.

Another island grievance was caused at this time by a fall in the value of the legal currency, livre tournois. Otto's officials claimed payment of moneys due in 'strong' livres, whereas the islanders argued that if the currency had fallen in value, and Otto was paid in 'weak' livres, Otto must lose. The argument was referred to the King in Council, but the case was decided against the islanders.

Thus it must have seemed that their rights were continually under attack, and their grievances were never dealt with. This unresolved situation continued until 1320. Then as a result of a most urgent petition to the King, complaining of extortion, imprisonment and other illegal acts by the officials, a new inquiry was set up, consisting of William de Bourne, Nicholas de Chesney and John de Carteret. The presence of men with island names suggests that the King had agreed that no officials should be members of these inquiries. Certainly this court should have satisfied the islanders, for it declared in favour of the islanders' privileges, it fined some of the officials and ordered them to return property they had illegally acquired, and it condemned and hanged one of the most notorious, Gautier de la Salle.

This de la Salle, a former bailiff, had been involved in a *cause célèbre*. Some years before one of the monks of the little priory on Lihou had been murdered, and the King's officers, among them a Ranulph Gautier, went to Lihou to arrest the murderer. But Ranulph Gautier slew the murderer, and after seeking sanctuary at St. Sampson's, he abjured and fled the island of Guernsey. Eventually he won the King's pardon and returned. But Gautier de la Salle arranged his imprisonment in Castle Cornet, where with an accomplice, William l'Enginour, he first tortured Ranulph Gautier and then murdered him.

This crime was proved to the justices and Gautier de la Salle was taken away to the gibbet in St. Andrews, passing on his way the Bailiff's Cross which still stands, incised in a stone by the roadside. His property was forfeit to the Crown, and the area is known to this day as Ville au Roi.

But the islanders were not satisfied with this success. They further petitioned the justices that the great Otto himself should be dismissed. This request was beyond the scope of the justices' commission, so they referred the petition to London. To London, too, was sent an advocate by the islanders to put their own case. Now Otto was really on the defensive, and he counter-attacked fiercely. His men beat up the advocate in the street, so that he was too frightened to put his case. Otto complained to the King, cunningly pointing out that his Lordship of the Isles was only for life, and that such action by the islanders and by the 1320 justices reduced the King's prerogative and rights.

Otto's views prevailed with Edward, who had the records brought to him and publicly quashed the whole proceedings of the Assize.

Deadlock now followed. Gerard d'Oron, Otto's nephew, was sent over to Guernsey as sub-warden, to carry out the King's orders and resume all the lands, liberties and rents which the previous assize had transferred. There was open revolt and he was forced to flee to Sark. After four months he returned, put his case before the Royal Court, and at the same time attempted to dismiss the bailiff. The bailiff promptly threw him into prison. By this time a new set of justices had arrived from England to hold a fresh assize. To them the islanders explained that their resistance was based on the fact that in d'Oron's commission there was no mention of 'the laws and customs of the Islands'.

To this day, when a new Lieutenant-Governor presents his royal warrant to the island Bailiff, the Court and the States, and takes the oath, he swears to maintain and guard the privileges, liberties and ancient customs accorded to the inhabitants of the Islands by their royal rulers over many hundreds of years. Only when he has sworn does the shout arise: 'Dieu sauve le Roi.'

Otto himself came over in 1323, to see what was happening on his rebellious 'estate', but nothing could break down the stubborn insistence of the islanders on their customs and privileges. There was a further development. In this struggle the advocates often used the phrase 'the community of the islands'; a feeling of nationhood, of oneness among the bailiff, jurats, seigneurs and people was being created.

The islanders were in an ugly mood, so that when the Prior of St. Michael du Valle tried to abolish the age-old custom of the people of marching in annual procession round the church, there was a riot.

In 1330 the young Edward III announced his intention to govern for himself, setting aside the unpopular regency of his mother Isabella and her lover Mortimer. In the forefront of his mind lay his claim to the throne of France, for he was the nephew of Charles IV; Philip of Valois, the other claimant, was only a cousin. In the meantime Edward endeavoured to set his kingdom in order. He sent over new justices to the Islands to hold yet another assize.

This time the resistance was more serious still. Before the justices could arrive in Guernsey, a meeting was held in Jersey, in St. Helier Priory, attended by twenty-three leading men from both islands, at which they bound themselves on oath to resist any interference with their ancient liberties. They then crossed to Guernsey to meet the justices; which they did, backed by a crowd of five hundred men. They formally protested that 'their customs belonged to them alone, that the King had no right to modify them or impose new ones, and that they were ready to defend them with their lives'.

The crowd backed them up with threats and cries of 'Oui, Oui, Oui.' Eventually the two leaders, Laurent du Gaillard and John le Viner, were cited before the justices, but an island jury promptly acquitted them. The justices then, as so often before, adjourned their decision, and the case was transferred again to the King's Council.

Thirty years or more of oppression, extortion and lack of decision had brought the hitherto loyal islanders to the verge of rebellion.

Chapter 5

The Hundred Years War

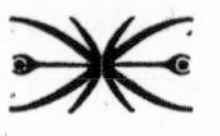

It was in this tense atmosphere that the French King appeared on the scene.

For the next hundred years and more the effects of the involvement of the Islands in the great struggle for power and spheres of influence between the Kings of England and the Kings of France were to be very great. On the one hand the islanders were to benefit, as it became increasingly clear that only if they were fairly treated, with due respect for their ancient privileges, could they be relied on to hold their island fortresses safely and loyally against the enemy. On the other hand, with their royal castles, and their havens as bases for English shipping, they were obvious targets for French attack, a challenge to the French Kings' desire to unify all the territories which they considered should be theirs. Whether, in the years of Edward III's ascendancy after Creçy and Henry V's after Agincourt, the French were in general on the defensive, or in the period of Edward's decline and of the Lancastrian leaders' struggles in the growing confusion of Henry VI's reign, the French were attacking in all sectors, the Islands lay in the Bay of Avranches apparently inviting French raids and French intrigues.

At the start the young King Edward III, who did not take kindly to vassalage in France and the continuing interference by Philip of France in the affairs of Aquitaine, was not aggressive, particularly as he was troubled by war with the Scots.

Yet the support which the French gave to the Scots made him realize that, until he had secured his rear from French attack, he could not finish with Scotland satisfactorily. This situation was emphasized by a raid on the Islands in 1336, by David Bruce, then a refugee in France. The report stated: 'David Bruce with other adherents has attacked Guernsey and Jersey, inhumanly committing arson, murder, and divers other atrocities.' In fact the main damage seems to have been to Sark and Alderney.

This raid had an important result in the Islands, emphasizing the growing harmony between the Government and the islanders. After the death in 1328 of the detested Otto, a new warden, John de Roches, was appointed, who had the unenviable task of putting things right. He found that Otto's men had let the castles and other defences decay, and with the full support of the English Government he had to repair the neglect. He tried to raise funds from any chattels that Otto might have left in the Islands; but Otto had left nothing. Repairs were carried out and the islanders were slightly conciliated by his honest and efficient government. It is doubtful whether he spent any time or money on the defences of Alderney or Sark; he is said to have reported that Alderney could not be defended and that Sark needed no defences.

Things had improved so much by the time of Bruce's raid that the islanders actually gave up one of their cherished privileges, that of not being forced to do any military service. They complied with the order of the next warden, de Ferrers, that all the men of the Islands capable of bearing arms should be levied. This was the foundation of the island militias, forces which had a continuous history until the militia regiments were disbanded in 1940.

There was further provocation from the French in 1337, when French privateers harassed the Islands, and went on to attack the English south coast. In August Edward issued his first definite defiance of Philip, styling him 'Philip who calls himself King of the French'. The Hundred Years War was in the process of breaking out, and there exposed to constant attack were the Islands, an outlying bastion of the English kingdom.

The first attack of the actual war was a raid by the French fleet under Admiral Behuchet, who sailed against Jersey—'On the morrow after the Annunciation he invaded the island with a great host and burnt every blade of corn and all the houses.' Though he overran the island he failed to take Gorey Castle, and sailed on to capture Castle Cornet and Sark and Alderney. The French King handed over the rule of the Islands to Robert Bertram, Marshal of France, who in the next year arrived in Jersey with a force of eight thousand men and fifty ships. With this show of strength he held the Islands and put a garrison in Castle Cornet, but Gorey Castle rejected his offer to confirm the Island's privileges if it would surrender. Anti-English feeling, arising from the bitter struggle for their rights, had not altogether died though; when the French forces withdrew, one of the jurats and a seigneur fled to France, forfeiting all rights in the island as traitors.

In 1340, an English fleet under Edward's command smashed the opposing Frenchmen with their Genoese and Spanish mercenaries at the battle of Sluys. After the battle Behuchet was hanged from his own masthead, like Eustace the Monk before him. Relief came to Guernsey when Walter de Weston led a force there which cleared the island, though Castle Cornet on its island stronghold held out, with a garrison of one French knight and eighty men.

The importance of the Islands to Edward in his plans for war was increased at this time. The death of John of Brittany removed a friend, whose ports had been open to English shipping, and when Philip of Valois's nephew claimed the Duchy, the Islands became even more vital as bases and harbours of refuge.

The immediate effect was a strenuous effort to recapture the royal Castle Cornet. It was closely besieged by English-

3 Mont Orgueil Castle, Jersey

4 L'Eperquerie, Sark

men, Jerseymen and Guernseymen, with Guernsey seamen manning a barge to try to stop supplies getting through. At last, after seven years, in 1345 a combined operation with English men-at-arms, island fighters and seamen retook the castle after a three-day assault. The French captain and the whole of the garrison were slain.

One reason for the successful defence by the French over this long period was that they improved the defensive walls and tower protecting the entrance, building them up with mortar made from sea-shells found on the islet.

But the vital strategic importance of the Islands, coupled with evidence that a few had been dealing as traitors with the enemy, had a more lasting result—the conclusion of their struggle for their rights.

On the 10th July 1341 the King suddenly confirmed the privileges of the Islands *in toto*.

'Considering how faithfully the beloved men of our Isles have ever maintained their loyalty towards the Kings of England, and how much they have suffered in defence of their Islands and of our rights and honour, we concede for ourselves and our heirs that they hold and retain all privileges, immunities and customs granted by our forebears or of other legal competency and that they enjoy them freely without molestation by ourselves, our heirs and our officers.' The document was rushed through and did not in fact specify the particular rights, customs and privileges for which they had struggled so hard and long. That was to be dealt with on a later occasion; but the question did not arise for the remainder of the Middle Ages.

The government of the Islands had now evolved to a form which lasted for centuries more or less unchanged. Under the warden there were in each island officers who helped in the administration and defence. The most important was the Receiver, who was directly responsible for the collection and accountancy of the revenue. Humbler men were the castle porters, who acted as gaolers, and at Castle Cornet the two boatmen. The castle also had a chaplain—

'because our men from England who are there cannot be without a chaplain who can understand and speak their tongue'.

But at the centre of island life was the Royal Court, a court each for Jersey, Guernsey, Alderney and Sark. Over each presided the Bailiffs of Jersey and Guernsey, and the Prévôts of Alderney and Sark. The Jurats gave judgment, but the bailiff was responsible for initiating proceedings and for seeing that the judgment was carried out. As he was dealing with island law and it was by now island custom that he should be a 'resident', he and the Court gradually became effectively independent.

In the war Edward III had now turned to the offensive, and went on to reach the pinnacle of his glory with the victory of Creçy and the capture of Calais. This stronghold gave the English fleets control of the eastern Channel as the Channel Islands did of the western, and the pressure on the Islands relaxed.

But a new and deadly enemy attacked—the Black Death. Little is know of its devastation, but in Jersey only two of the parish rectors did not die, and the death-rate among the Islands' fishermen was so heavy that the King waived his claim to the taxes on fish.

It was just as well that the King paid some attention to the Guernsey defences at this time. He ordered the construction of a fort, Tour Beauregard, on the height commanding the southern approaches to the town, to which was allotted a garrison under the command of a captain. He also ordered that the town should be fortified with a strong wall, running from Tour Beauregard by Clifton to Tour Gand. There is however no evidence that this work was done, and it is a reasonable guess that the island's funds were not sufficient for this major work.

In 1356 the French mounted another raid. They were on the defensive in Normandy, where the English held most of the strongholds. But a French force slipped away across the sea and captured Castle Cornet. The reaction from Jersey was swift. De Carteret of St. Ouen's, with the bailiff and other leading men, raised a relief force, which after suffering some casualties retook the castle and collected 80,000 florins in ransom money from the French commander.

In the course of the action they took and executed as a traitor a Guernseyman, Guillaume le Feyvre. This act brought out inter-insular rivalry, and incurred the wrath of the Guernsey bailiff and jurats. The Jersey 'rescuers' were judged guilty of murder and put in the dungeon. It was two years before they were pardoned 'in regard to the arduous task they had performed in recovering the castle'.

With the signing of the Treaty of Bretigny in 1360, by which the French recognized Edward's claim to Aquitaine and gave up all claims to the Islands, the war temporarily died down. But in Spain and Brittany the fighting never ceased. It was the era of Calverley and Hawkwood, mercenary captains of such companies as the White Company, whose trade was war. France too was led by a competent king, Charles V, and the great Bertrand du Guesclin.

So it was not long before the threat of attack on the Islands was to arise again. But it was not only war that made life hazardous at that time. A great hurricane swept Jersey, pouring the sea over the Manor of Bequette, in the Bay of St. Ouen's, and engulfing not only the house but the surround forest too for ever. Further inland men and beasts were slain by hailstones.

Local rivalries, too, were liable to flare up. Philip de Barentin, Seigneur of Rozel in Jersey, was accused by his relatives of being a leper. This was quite a possibility as the disease had been brought back by Crusaders, and there were lazarettos, maladreries, set aside in Jersey and Guernsey. His relatives went to law to secure a judgment that he was unfit to hold his property. To thwart them he sold the estate. But while the case dragged on, his wife Madame de Barentin stayed alone at the manor. Tongues wagged and spread rumours of her association with the seigneur of the nearby manor of Trinity, Jehannet de St. Martin. She called her sons and cried: 'Jehannet de St. Martin has called me an adultress. Avenge this insult. Such slanderers ought to have their tongues torn out.' The Barentin sons laid an ambush for St. Martin, caught him and tore out his tongue by the roots. They eventually escaped to France by seeking sanctuary and following the Sanctuary Track to a boat.

But there were more important affairs to worry about. In 1372, after the French fleets had been sailing more or less unchecked in the Channel, reports reached Guernsey that a French force was gathering at Le Havre for a big raid. The Guernsey garrison managed to get reinforcements of eighty men-at-arms and archers from friendly Normandy before the attacking fleet arrived. This attack, which is recorded in Froissart's Chronicles, and in the only extant Guernsey ballad, a ballad with the title 'La descente des Aragousais', was commanded by Yvain de Galles (Owen of Wales). He was the son of a Welsh Prince put to death by Edward III, and as one of the 'Disinherited' was a deadly enemy of England.

With his force of six hundred men he landed at Vazon Bay, and slowly drove back the armed islanders until a pitched battle took place above the town, at a site still known as 'Battle Lane'. Although reinforced by the men-at-arms, the islanders suffered heavy casualties, eight hundred dead according to one authority, and were driven into the town and the defences of Beauregard. Yvain moved round to try to take Castle Cornet, but after a skirmish he re-embarked and sailed to St. Sampson's. One story goes that there he besieged Aymon Rose, the sub-warden, in the Vale Castle.

Mais Aymon Rose retranché
Au puissant Château de l'Archange
Dit qu'il serait avant tranché
Que de se rendre à gent estrange.

The stalemate was finally resolved by the Prior of the Vale, who persuaded Yvain to leave the island in return for a ransom. To help in the collection of this the island women threw in their ear-rings and other jewellery.

There is an old tradition about this raid: that the islanders tried to make a primitive cannon by hollowing out a tree-trunk and filling it with explosive, but no one could be induced to fire it until a child, lured by the promise of a cake, set a touch-light to it.

In the following year there came a more dangerous adversary, du Guesclin, who with the Duc de Bourbon left the siege of Brest and sailed across the sea with two thousand men-at-arms and six hundred bowmen. He landed in Jersey, and after overrunning the island attacked Gorey Castle. The defenders, including the bailiff and the jurats, who had taken refuge there, were driven back into the keep. From there they negotiated with du Guesclin, who had with him no equipment for a siege, and handed over hostages and a ransom by instalments. Leaving a force in control of the Jersey countryside, du Guesclin sailed on to Sark and to Guernsey. In both islands he did much damage to mills and houses, and possibly collected a ransom from Guernsey. This rather discreditable affair and the crisis which followed led to the dismissal of the warden. The Bailiff of Jersey spent some time in the Tower of London. However, one gets a glimpse of the English genius for improvisation in an emergency. Fighting men were appointed as wardens of each island, with a set of officials to support each of them, but with one man, Thomas of Appleby, responsible for collecting all the revenues and for supplying the soldiers with the sinews of war.

Although, as the chronicler's obituary of Edward III remarked, 'unprofitable things continued long after,' the Islands were fortunate in their new warden, Sir Hugh Calverley. He held the command of both islands for sixteen years, and had only one raid to deal with. This took place in 1380, when a French fleet under Admiral de Vienne arrived to attack Jersey with two thousand men-at-arms. The island and Gorey Castle surrendered, as did Castle

Cornet, and the Islands were granted by the Regent to Vienne as his personal possession. But Calverley managed to raise a relieving force and expel the Frenchman. This time the Jersey bailiff was kept in prison for four years, and nearly paid the penalty for treason.

While Sir Hugh Calverley had no further serious trouble from French raiders during his period of office, the claims of the Bishop of Coutances caused great complications. As has already been explained, the Islands came under him for ecclesiastical discipline and control, and this fact had caused friction. He cited islanders to appear at his court in Coutances, and the King for once supported the islanders' privilege of not being tried out of their island. The Bishop countered this by creating local Dean's Courts, for ecclesiastical cases, which clashed with the island Royal Courts.

A much greater problem was set in 1378, when the Papal Schism occurred, that is to say the election by the Italians of Pope Urban VI at Rome, and the election by the French of Pope Clement VII at Avignon. Naturally England supported Urban VI, but the Bishop of Coutances was an ardent Clementine. The Deans and many of the parish rectors were also pro-Clement, and Calverley could only solve the problem by banishing the Deans and importing the Bishop of Nantes, an Urbanite, to control the Islands' churches.

Otherwise the Islands managed to escape the violence and uncertainty of the unhappy reign of Richard II. Only in the negotiations for his marriage to the young French Princess Isabelle did a dangerous threat appear. Her father pressed for the surrender of the Islands as an integral part of Normandy. Although the marriage took place and a so-called truce to last thirty years was made, this clause was not agreed.

A strange contrast to this disturbed time, when the Roman Catholic Church was split between Pope and anti-Pope, and when Wycliffe and his Lollards were preaching their reforming doctrines through the length and breadth of England, occurred in Guernsey. There one of the Henries,

Nicholas, founded a chantry chapel of St. Apolline, for masses for his soul, for that of his wife, Philippa, and for the souls of their ancestors, benefactors and Christian people generally for ever. The King Richard II, too, founded the Convent of Franciscan Friars, Les Cordeliers, above the town, on the site where later Elizabeth College was to be founded.

A number of these friars, wishing to serve God 'in quietude and peace', moved to Herm, but the hostility of the local fishermen soon drove them away again from the little island.

The official truce continued during Henry IV's reign, but so did the endemic war at sea between the English and the French with their Castilian allies. From this came an attack on Jersey in 1406, when a pirate fleet of Bretons and Castilians, strengthened by a thousand men-at-arms from St. Malo, sailed on a raid. On the sands before St. Helier they fought a fierce pitched battle, which was vividly described by the standard-bearer of the Castilians, Pero Nino. The Jerseymen resisted stoutly, but were driven back. Then the raiders, who had suffered heavy losses, learnt of the yet uncaptured strongpoints in the island, and compromised for a ransom of 10,000 gold crowns. To the islanders' relief they sailed away.

But there was no relief for Sark a few years later. A French force swooped down and pillaged the island, massacring the entire population. Only the monks, whose order had lasted there quietly, if precariously, for so many centuries, were spared, on condition that they moved to France. Pirates, smugglers and wreckers gradually filtered into the empty island, a natural fortress from which they could take toll of passing ships.

Obviously with the accession of the young and ambitious Henry V the Islands were drawn into his schemes against France. The first move to affect them was both national and financial, his attack on the alien priories. French abbeys had held great possessions in the Islands for centuries, many

Frenchmen held benefices, and the drain of money into enemy hands was considerable. With the support of the English Parliament he ordered that all these lands should revert to the Crown, which also took control of the tithes and advowsons of the parish churches. Exception was only made for the lands held by the Abbey of Marmoutiers. This seizure caused great changes in the Islands, but there is no record of any active opposition. In fact it was clearly a gain, for it virtually removed the last of the powerful absentee landholders. No doubt islanders with influence acquired portions of the forfeited estates. It seems probable that the Fief Sausmarez in Castel, Guernsey, was added to when the Le Marchant family acquired bits of the old lands of the Priories of St. Michael du Valle and Lihou.

Other benefits came to the islanders from Henry's successful campaigns in Normandy. They made their contribution by serving gladly in his armies, and by providing ships and seamen for the siege of Cherbourg, and for the long but vain attempt to reduce the fortress Abbey of Mont St. Michel. Three Jerseymen were granted lands by Henry as a reward for their war service.

The main reward was the increased safety of the area, so that trade revived, helped by safe conducts from the admirals on both sides. The merchants and farmers of Jersey and Guernsey got profit from the King's ships which called in for revictualling and paid good money for fish and corn and butter.

A side-effect of this increased safety and prosperity was the desire to go on pilgrimage. It is recorded that in one year sixty licences were issued to islanders intending to travel on pilgrimage to St. James of Compostella. In Jersey itself money was spent to enlarge the parish churches; some had a chancel added, others a new and loftier nave.

Another interesting result of this time, when the Bay of Avranches was more or less an English sea, was the emigration from Guernsey and Normandy of families to Alderney. These families, Olliviers, Le Cocqs, Gaudions, Herivels, and others, helped to swell to about seven hundred a population which had been much reduced by the fierce French attacks of previous years.

After 1422, when Henry V and the mad King of France both died, the Islands were concerned much less in international affairs. The Lordship of the Isles was granted in succession to three important men, the Regent, John, Duke of Bedford; Humphrey of Gloucester, his younger and more turbulent brother; and to Richard Neville, the great Earl of Warwick. These three men were regarded by the English Government as absolute rulers of the Islands, with quasi-royal privileges; but it does not appear that they played any active part in island life or government.

The Islands continued to be a base for the English fleet as the French, under the inspired leadership of Joan of Arc, gradually drove the English armies from territory after territory. Island seamen went to help in attacks on French strongholds, such as Granville, and there were French raids too. John Paston, in the Paston Letters, is told:

'The Frenchmen hafe be afore the Isles of Gersey and Guernsey, and a grate many of hem, and VC (500) be taken and slayn by men of the seyd trew Isles.'

But by 1450 the whole of Normandy was lost, and soon only Calais remained of all the English possessions on the French mainland. As French fleets controlled the seas, it cost John Nanfan, the new warden, the sum of 250 crowns to purchase a safe conduct from the French admiral for his passage to the Islands. Nanfan was a veteran soldier, who had fought under Henry V at Agincourt, but he also had links with the Yorkist party in England. So for eight years he managed to keep the Islands out of the dogfight of the Wars of the Roses.

The Islands could not be kept out of English politics permanently. There is a record in Guernsey about an estate called Le Franc-Fief Gallicien. The tenants enjoyed in future centuries exemption from certain dues because in 1459 their ancestors, seamen plying to Exmouth, helped the Earl of

March, later to be Edward IV, along with the Earl of Warwick and their followers, to get away from the Lancastrians after the defeat of Ludlow, and to escape to the island, on their way to Calais.

In 1461 Gorey Castle was surprised and captured by a French force commanded by Sir Jean Carbonnel, a cousin of the Count of Maulevrier. This Count was a remarkable man, a poet and an experienced soldier, who was then Grand Sénéschal of Normandy, and first cousin of Marguerite of Anjou, Henry VI's Queen. The timing of this attack suggests that she and Count Maulevrier were planning to secure the Islands as a refuge for the Lancastrian royal family, and for Maulevrier to be appointed Lord of the Isles. Some suspicion fell on Nanfan, but a more likely person to have left a postern-gate open for the French was the Attorney-General, Guillaume de St. Martin, whose family were staunch Lancastrians. A further clue was that Nanfan's lieutenant had imprisoned two of the St. Martins in Castle Cornet for two years without taking legal action against them.

Jersey had to endure a French occupation for seven years. In fact the bailiff signed documents as 'Bailiff under the High and Mighty Lord, the Count of Maulevrier, Lord of the Isles'. Jersey as a whole seems to have accepted the change of ruler, especially as all the existing institutions were approved and confirmed, and a Public Register was established for the transfer of property.

But there were pro-English families, and for one of them the acting-Governor Carbonnel set a trap. He had captured a young man named John Haverford from a foraging party of the Earl of Warwick's which had put in from Calais. This young man he treated well, and let out on parole, so that he got to know socially the Seigneur of Rozel, Renaud Lemprière and his English wife Katherine. Lemprière, as a seigneur and a jurat, was an influential man, who kept open house at his manor and was keenly interested in fishing, chess and tennis.

In August 1463 Carbonnel arrested Lemprière and the Rector of St. Martins, Thomas le Hardy, on a charge of conspiring with Guernseymen to recapture the castle. The main witness for the prosecution was John Haverford, who testified that Le Hardy had asked him at confession if he would help, and that Lemprière had offered him 100 crowns to leave the sally-port open. Katherine was cross-examined for a day and a half, but denied it all 'as she hoped for Paradise'. The accusations seem finally to have been dropped, but Le Hardy forfeited his estate of Méleches.

In spite of Civil War in France Carbonnel continued to hold Jersey in the name of the Duchy of Normandy, though his grip on the western part of the island may have weakened. For de Carteret, the Seigneur of St. Ouen's, seems to have joined the resistance, and only escaped arrest by the French when his horse jumped a sunken lane, eighteen feet deep and twenty-two feet wide, to get away to his manor and safety.

At last in 1468 relief came. Sir Richard Harliston, the Yorkist vice-admiral, sailed to Guernsey, and from there secretly landed at Plemont, Jersey, in the night and made contact with de Carteret. Later he returned with a fleet and troops from Guernsey, linked up with de Carteret's local forces, and together they advanced stealthily along the north coast. By dawn the castle, which was considered impregnable with its culverin and cannon, was surrounded, and the fleet blockaded it from the sea.

Although Carbonnel was relieved by one ship from Normandy with archers and supplies of biscuits, dried cod and cider, he eventually surrendered after a siege of nineteen weeks, and marched out with the honours of war. 'Sir Richard and the Seigneur of St. Ouen's and the leading men of the island entered the castle with great joy and placed the King's banners on every tower.'

There was even one occasion when islanders actively intervened in the Yorkist-Lancastrian struggle in England. Walsh, the Seigneur of St. Germains, Jersey, a big landowner, transported his tenants to the mainland to fight for the renegade Warwick the King-Maker against Edward IV. The armies met at Barnet, and there Warwick and Walsh were slain. The luckless Jerseymen tried to get away to Southampton and the safety of a boat, but they were recognized and all were hanged as traitors.

One outcome of Edward IV's final triumph was the official appointment of the able Harliston as Governor of the Islands. Edward also confirmed all the Islands' ancient customs and privileges, in recognition of the cost to the islanders, nearly £3,000, of their action against the French. The greatest benefit however that this practical ruler bestowed on them was secured in 1483, the year of his death. He made an agreement with the King of France that, if there should occur further war between the two countries, the Islands should be neutral.

In the next year the Pope Sixtus IV set his seal to this agreement, with a Bull of Neutrality, in which he pronounced 'a sentence of anathema and eternal damnation with confiscation of goods on all who shall land in the islands to burn, plunder and murder the inhabitants, or shall carry out such crimes within sight of the islands as far as human eye shall reach.'

The Islands had managed to struggle through a long and stormy period, and could hope for a more peaceful and prosperous, if less exciting, future. They had succeeded in preserving their institutions and customs from undue interference and pressure from England. They had even extended their rights by successful agitation. An important example of this process was their long struggle to obtain exemption from English customs dues. When Edward I had laid down that these were to be paid by aliens only, they had immediately objected that they were not aliens. After sixty years of agitation they got their way, exemption from the dues on the ground that, though they were not denizens, they were not aliens, and therefore were 'reputed citizens'.

It was very human of them to wish to be English when it paid, but to be Normans when it did not. Underlying it really was a strong sense of their own identity. This common consciousness made one further important contribution during this period, the evolution of deliberative and legislative assemblies, known as The States. In the weak and often anarchical condition of the central government, The States, assemblies where the bailiff and the jurats were joined by some of the fief-holders, the clergy and the constables from the parishes to form a representative body, could get things done. By stressing that the duties of the officials were more to the islanders than to the King, and by petitions of 'the community' for royal authority to carry out certain acts or to raise the necessary money, they started on the path which led from royal administration to real self-government.

Chapter 6

The Tudors and the Calvinists: 1485—1630

WHEN the cautious and experienced Henry of Richmond defeated Richard III at Bosworth Field, it was the dawn of a new era, not only for England but also for the Islands. He had to find a compromise policy between the extremes of absolutism practised by Richard II and Edward IV, and the anarchy of the baronial exploitation of the feeble Lancastrian government. This policy evolved into the firm paternalist control of the Tudors, by which the Sovereign and the Council ordered all the affairs of the kingdom, while at the same time respecting the rights and feelings of the people.

There is a tradition that Henry Tudor landed in Jersey a year or so before his victory at Bosworth. He had sailed from Brittany to join up with his followers at Poole, but a great storm scattered his fleet. His ship alone put in at Jersey, and he took shelter with a Le Hardy. A monument to Sir Thomas Hardy in Westminster Abbey states 'His ancestor Clement le Hardy sheltered Henry and was rewarded with the office of Bailiff when Henry won the Crown'.

So he would have known about Harliston, the Yorkist Governor, whom he confirmed in office at his accession. Very early in his reign too he confirmed the charters, privileges and liberties of the Islands.

But Harliston had not given up hope of the Yorkist cause; when he found the Jersey seigneurs were lukewarm, he retreated into Gorey (Mont Orgueil) Castle, and there he was besieged for a few months. Though he had previously strengthened the fortifications and built a platform for cannon, he had no fleet and was forced to surrender.

After the departure of Harliston, who was to land in support of Perkin Warbeck's rising and to die in exile, Henry took the first steps in the reorganization of the Islands' government. He extinguished the claims of the old nobility to the Lordship of the Isles, by persuading the ancient Countess of Warwick, Anne de Beauchamp, to renounce 'the islands and lordship of Jernesey and Guernesey and the castles and manors of Gurry, Cornet, Sark, Erme and Aureney in the island aforesaid'. He also appointed two Governors, one for Guernsey, a second for Jersey. The Jersey appointment was Matthew Baker, a companion of Henry's in exile. According to the chronicler, 'Baker was extremely peevish, malicious and terribly vindictive,' and he soon alienated the island leaders by his high-handed actions. The spokesman for the island in appeals to the Privy Council was Philippe de Carteret, who had married Harliston's daughter. So Baker planned to ruin him.

He arranged for one of his own men, Le Boutellier, to drop a forged letter—in which de Carteret offered to betray Gorey Castle to the French—in a lane. As Baker rode that way to the court he had the letter picked up, and with it he challenged de Carteret, a jurat. De Carteret denied all knowledge of the letter. Baker's next move was an extraordinary one, for he revived the ancient practice of Trial by Battle. Le Boutellier threw down his gauntlet and offered to prove that de Carteret lied. De Carteret, who knew le Boutellier as a criminal, whom he himself had once saved from the gallows, refused to fight with such a man. But the Lancastrian bailiff, le Hardy, ordered that both men should be held in the castle until St. Lawrence's day, the date fixed for the battle.

To ensure success, the hefty le Boutellier was well exercised and fed, while de Carteret was kept on bread and water in the lowest dungeon. A second insurance measure was taken: hidden trenches were dug in the field of battle to hamper de Carteret on the day. Finally to check any plea by de Carteret to England, Baker forbade any boat to leave the island, and he himself set sail for England and the King's presence to make his case absolutely cast-iron.

Baker had reckoned without de Carteret's wife, Margaret. She had only recently had a baby, yet she persuaded a fisherman to carry her across to Guernsey. From there a friendly jurat, de Beauvoir, carried her across to Poole in his own sloop. As she reached the quay she saw Baker ahead of her, but a hailstorm drove him to shelter, and she was able to slip past unobserved. She raced on to Sheen Palace, and there Bishop Foxe took her into the presence of the King. So ably did she plead that Henry forbade the Trial by Battle, and reserved the case for the judgment of the Council. However Margaret had not yet won. She had to get back to Jersey before the date for the battle. Her luck held, and she managed to board a boat at Southampton which landed her in Jersey on the eve of St. Lawrence. The King's order, sealed with the Great Seal, was sufficient authority for the bailiff, who released de Carteret.

As a result, Baker was removed from office, but not before he had ended the career of the bailiff. It was proved that le Hardy had kept for himself some tuns of wine from a Spanish wreck cast up on Crown property. For this embezzlement he was thrown into the castle dungeon 'where at last he died, covered with lice and vermin'.

Although Henry was a realist and had no wish to revive England's continental policy, he valued the Islands for their link with Normandy, and for their strategic position and he wanted the islanders to be well-governed and contented. He therefore carried the reorganization of the Islands' government a stage further in 1495, by an Order in Council, which was strictly for Jersey only, but applied in fact to both the large islands. These regulations laid down the Governor's duties as regards the defences and garrisons, and stipulated the King's right to levy customs and to demand a day's work a year from the islanders on the defences.

The Governor's powers in relation to the islanders were defined: he was not to interfere in any judicial procedure, or to imprison in a treason case. The King, not the Governor, was alone to appoint the bailiff, the dean, the vicomte, and the procureur. The rules for the election and duties of the jurats were laid down more clearly, and any dispute between the jurats and the Governor was to be referred immediately to the Privy Council. By these provisions he hoped that the Islands would be efficiently defended, that the islanders would receive justice, and that there would be peace and harmony between the English officials and the island aristocracies.

In the last resort the success of his regulations depended on the calibre of the individual Governor, who had a very difficult task. He was the King's Captain, responsible for the royal castles and the Islands' defence and for the collection of the royal revenue to sustain it. He was also the interpreter of the orders of the King and his Council to the islanders, but the islanders had the right of direct appeal to the King and Council, and it grew to be the tradition of the Tudor Councils that they were prepared to devote much time and care to considering individual cases and matters which on the surface seemed quite trivial.

Henry VII followed up this constitutional reform with two other practical steps. He extracted a papal bull from Alexander Borgia, which transferred the Islands from the See of Coutances to that of Winchester. In theory this corrected an anomaly, but Winchester was far away and for the next fifty years the Bishop of Coutances continued to exercise his rights more or less unchallenged.

As Governor of Jersey Henry appointed a Southampton merchant, Thomas Overay. Overay had a successful term of office, and won high praise from everyone for the encouragement he gave to business with French and English merchants.

After a few years it was discovered that one reason for Overay's popularity was that 'he let royal domains at rents below their real value'. He was therefore replaced in 1500 by a boyhood friend of Henry's, Sir Hugh Vaughan, a handsome swashbuckling Welshman, who was reputed to have killed his opponent in a tournament at Richmond. Vaughan was a high-handed, violent and masterful man, who stirred up great opposition. He was reported to be quite unscrupulous in his greed; if he coveted an estate, he was liable to send for the title-deeds and to tear off the seals. Another accusation was made by the chronicler—'He gave himself up to wenching and became so lecherous that he would rape young girls by force, so that they dared not walk alone in the lanes.'

By 1513 the bailiff, Lemprière, was driven to cross to England to lay complaints before the young Henry VIII, who appointed two Commissioners to investigate the state of affairs. Vaughan anticipated their arrival by dismissing the bailiff and appointing Helier de Carteret in his place. He then overawed the Commissioners, whose findings completely whitewashed him, and he was left master of the island.

In 1519 his greed led him to go too far. He claimed Trinity Manor as forfeit to the Crown, on the grounds of the treason of the seigneur, Lemprière, with the French sixty years before, ignoring the fact that the seigneur had been pardoned long ago. Helier de Carteret, the bailiff, was a relation, and when he was about to dismiss the case, Vaughan threatened to run him through with his sword. This attempted intimidation led de Carteret to go to England. There he won favour with the young King for his charm and for his skill with the bow and arquebus, but he could make no headway with his summons against Vaughan, for Vaughan had close links with the powerful Chancellor, Cardinal Wolsey. There is a record of a gift from Vaughan to Wolsey of five hundred gallons of wine. Certain it is that every time for twelve years de Carteret's case came up, Wolsey adjourned it and passed to the next. Further de Carteret was compelled by Wolsey's order to attend every meeting of the Council and so was kept fruitlessly in London, with less and less resources as he had lost his post as bailiff and the revenue from his manor.

At last in 1528 de Carteret challenged Wolsey directly in the Star Chamber, shouting loudly: 'Sir, I entreat you for justice.' Angrily Wolsey threatened to send him to the Fleet Prison, but still de Carteret spoke out. When he stated that he had the island seal and was not as Wolsey said 'unfit to hold any rule in the island', Wolsey broke off the sitting in a rage.

This stalwart opposition must have moved the Cardinal, for later he and de Carteret met privately and Wolsey admitted: 'In truth I think you have been wronged.' On the first day of the next legal term de Carteret was restored to his office of bailiff and to his manor, and returned to Jersey, reconciled on the surface to Vaughan.

Retribution on Vaughan followed soon after, for his patron, the Cardinal, fell from power in October 1529. A flood of petitions poured in from Jersey, and a Commission was appointed to look into the charges against Vaughan. This Commission consisted of four men, two of them islanders, and after a very conscientious inquiry, they came down heavily against Vaughan. Many were his misdeeds. He was shown to have acted violently, even beating three men to death, to have neglected the castle defences, and to have extorted money and property. The general impression remains that he had ruled the island as a tyrant, and after the Commission's report he retired, to reappear as the Bailiff of Westminster, dealing energetically with the plague.

Although Vaughan had terrorized them the Jerseymen had triumphed in the end, and there is little doubt that this case made an impression on the Council in England. They came to have more respect for islanders who were so tenacious of their rights, and for a champion such as de Carteret who was so stubborn and fearless in his opposition.

From this time the personality and aims of Henry VIII increasingly dominated the scene, as in his search for a divorce he swept away Wolsey, defied the Pope, and drove on to political Reformation. His policy, carried through by the ruthless Cromwell and approved by the Seven Years Parliament, naturally affected the Islands. There his religious measures caused little concern or difference, as much of the work had already been done by Henry V when he confiscated the alien priories. The Governor of Guernsey arranged for the foreign friars to cross to Normandy and claimed possession for the Crown of the Franciscan friary buildings.

However the hostility of the Pope, and the possibility of attack or invasion by foreign Catholics, made the Council conscious of the increased threat to the Islands. Though they were technically neutral, they were an important centre for the collection of military intelligence, and if not well defended, might be seized by pirates or privateers as a base. Henry decided to use some of the monastic funds he had acquired in improving coastal defences, for the medieval royal castles were now faced with attack by cannon. In particular he was advised of the threat to Castle Cornet, 'the key and centre of the Isles', as the Dean of Guernsey later described it, and instructions were sent to the Governor, Sir Peter Mewtis, to modernize it. Under the supervision of John Rogers, the King's chief engineer, a bastion and artillery emplacement, called Mewtis Bulwark, was constructed at a cost of £492 17s. 10d.

In Jersey, too, improvements were made to Mont Orgueil Castle, in particular the construction of the great tower to face the threat from the dominating hill opposite. This tower was named Somerset Tower, after Edward Seymour, Jane Seymour's brother, who held the Governorship from 1537 to 1550. His lieutenant, Cornish, the King's godson, had a difficult task in trying to raise funds for this project, and for the squat tower on an islet off St. Aubin's harbour. His purveyor was accused by the islanders of requisitioning too much material for this work, and of paying too little for it.

In the last year of Henry's reign work was begun on a strong fortress to cover the approaches to Longy Bay in Alderney, which was intended as a naval base. Seymour, by now Protector Somerset, had the work pushed on, and a labour force of two hundred was sent over as well as a further two hundred men as garrison. While the fort's walls were beginning to rise, the Government's fears for the Islands were proved justified, as Henry III of France sent a strong force to seize Sark. The only inhabitants were seven smugglers, so that the French captain, Bruel, had no difficulty in landing four hundred men. As most of these were ex-convicts, his main task was to keep them on the island, and by 1551 his force had dwindled to ninety men.

There was little more objection to the Protestant measures of Edward VI's Council of Regency than there had been to Henry's English Catholicism. The Act for the suppression of Chantries, The Act of Uniformity, and Cranmer's Prayer Book of 1549, specially translated into French, were accepted. Only one or two rectors refused to submit, and a few laymen were convicted of privately attending mass.

The loudest outcry arose in Jersey where an order was promulgated that all the church bells, except for one in each parish, should be collected and sold to raise funds for the erection of new fortifications on the islet off St. Helier harbour. The superstitious felt justified when the ship carrying the bells foundered in the harbour; for centuries it was said that the bells could be heard ringing out before a storm.

By this date the religious views of some of the islanders were outstripping the political reformation. The driving force came from the Reform Movement in France. There wilder and fiercer spirits had taken up the ideas first put forward by Jacques le Févre. He was a gentle reformer, but his followers were driven by persecution and burnings into uncompromising, militant resistance to what they considered antichrist. Le Févre's French translations of the New Testament and religious tracts were spread through Normandy by colporteurs, and undoubtedly this underground movement spread to Jersey and thence to the other islands. The reforming party were helped too by trained Frenchmen, who were appointed as rectors 'to expound the Word of God to the people purely according to the Gospel'.

The lieutenant, Cornish, was dismissed soon after the fall of Protector Somerset, and Jersey was fortunate in the new Governor. He was Sir Hugh Poulet, a Somerset man, an able and high-minded leader and a keen reformer. He continued the dual task laid on him, of defending the island and of purging it of Popery.

But the accession of the devout Catholic, Queen Mary, altered the situation radically. The Latin services were restored, the prominent Reforming rectors fled, and those rectors who had married had to put away their wives. Poulet bided his time and handled the difficult situation very skilfully. He appointed his brother, a Catholic, as Dean, and thus had some control over the possible excesses of the Church authorities. This was wise, as many leading islanders refused to give up their Reformed practice and found ways and means of taking the Sacrament in a Reformed service. Some used to slip away across the sea to St. Lô in Normandy for the service.

In Guernsey, where the Reformers were not so popular and many of the leaders were Catholic at heart, Mary's reversal of the religious situation was accepted, and there was persecution. In 1556 a terrible deed was done. Three women, Catherine Cauchés and her two daughters, were convicted of heresy by the Dean, and condemned by the Royal Court to be burnt at the stake. As the flames rose one daughter gave birth to a baby boy and this little child was thrown back into the fire, on the orders of the bailiff, Helier Gosselin. A possible clue to the ferocity of this deed may be that both the bailiff and the dean, Amy, had held their posts during Edward's reign, and wished to parade their religious zeal, now that Mary had appointed a new Catholic Governor, Sir Leonard Chamberlain.

Mary's single-minded concern for her religion led her to neglect other aspects of policy. In 1553 a chance arose to liquidate the French occupation of Sark. A Flemish privateer, Adrian Crole, put in at Guernsey, and with the aid of local pilots, landed in Little Sark; crossing La Coupée, he caught the French sentries asleep and quickly forced the French surrender. His arrival at Mary's Court with this news and the suggestion of a reward only embarrassed the Government, which had signed a truce with the French. Crole received no reward, not even his expenses, and the whole affair was hushed up. Sark remained unclaimed and uninhabited.

Mary's tragic reign drew to its close—the nation despondent, the Treasury empty, Calais lost. As the Dean of Jersey, whose authority had been defied by his brother, Sir Hugh, took ship to England to appeal to the Queen, he was met as he sailed past La Corbière point by a boat from England. 'What news?' shouted his crew. 'Good news,' came the reply. 'Jezebel is dead.'

The young Queen Elizabeth, with her supremely able adviser, Sir William Cecil, faced many problems; the most pressing were the religious situation, the struggle with France, and the weak state of the finances. The Islands were directly concerned. In Jersey the strong hand of the Protestant Sir Hugh Poulet, supported by his son Amyas, ensured a calm transition. The Acts of Supremacy and Uniformity were put in force, and Jersey settled down to a Protestant régime, which satisfied many of the leading families, the de Carterets, the Lemprières.

But the situation in Guernsey was more difficult. There the Governor did not command much respect, the bailiff and a majority of the jurats were Catholics and the islanders were discontented, quarrelsome, and unwilling to contribute to the island's defences. Though religion was one cause of this situation—'the generality here mislike the late alterations in England', as the Governor reported to Cecil in 1562—commerce was a deeper cause. Guernsey merchants had developed by this date a greater overseas trade, particularly with France, than Jersey, and they feared that the religious changes would destroy the validity of the Bull of Neutrality. Local neutrality in Guernsey waters had been accepted by the French in the wars of Henry's and Somerset's time. But now, when it was treason to refer to a papal bull, would the French continue to agree to this local privilege?

Another interrelated problem, which influenced the islanders' attitude, was that of defence and the cost of paying for it. As John After, the Calvinist dean, reported to Cecil, 'They have long been preserved from invasion by privileges from England, patents from France, and bulls from Rome, so that they have no thought of danger.'

Already in 1560 the English Government had confirmed the island's charters and privileges, including that of trading with all persons, even the enemy, in time of war. But it became abundantly clear that the state of affairs in Guernsey must be closely examined.

Commissioners were appointed, at first to look into church property, for Elizabeth intended to use the money and rents partly for defence, partly for the establishment of a school. The resistance of the bailiff and the Catholic jurats to the inquiry and to the stable establishment of the Protestant Church led to the extension of the Commission's business. Catherine Cauchés's brother petitioned against the burning of his sister, and the guilty Bailiff Gosselin was dismissed from office. This did not overawe the rebellious jurats. They continued on their course, stirring up the people, using the money from the confiscated obits and church plate to bring writs against the Government, and hampering the officials and the Commission in every way.

The situation grew more tense as the Protestant party turned steadily to Calvinism. The influence and doctrine of Jean Calvin had gained an increasingly strong hold in France, especially in Normandy and Brittany, and from there, as the ultra-Catholic Guise family intensified their persecution, Calvinist, or Huguenot refugees started to escape to the Islands. Each refugee, who could address the islanders in their own tongue, was a missionary for his faith, and the number of converts steadily increased.

In Jersey one of the first was Amyas Poulet, who in 1562 appointed a Huguenot minister, Guillaume Morise, to be rector of the town church of St. Helier. 'At this supper', the chronicler records, 'Amyas Poulet, the lieutenant-governor, and the Seigneur of St. Ouen's and most of the leading gentry of the island were present. Afterwards Guillaume Morise ordained Elders and Deacons, and with the assent of the Lieutenant and the Jurats formed a Consistory with a good discipline.' In Calvin's system a Consistory was the Parish Church Council; above it was the Colloquy for a group of parishes, and above that the national Synod.

In Guernsey, likewise, a Consistory for the Town Church of St. Peter Port was established by another Huguenot refugee, Nicholas Baudouin, in 1563; he had been brought over to the island by William de Beauvoir, the leading Protestant Guernseyman, who was a friend and disciple of Calvin.

The establishment of these two centres of Presbyterianism met with considerable opposition. First the Bishop of Coutances struggled hard to maintain his threadbare claims. He had already been driven out of his own cathedral city, sitting on an ass with his face to the tail. But he came to London and demanded the fees due to him from the Islands. The Council ordered the disputed fees to be paid, but Guernsey refused to pay them. The position was cleared up in 1565, when the Council ordered the Islands to be united to the See of Winchester. The last rumblings from the Bishop were heard in 1580 when a rumour spread that he was recruiting an army to recover the Islands.

Elizabeth was scarcely more pleased with the Presbyterian system than the Bishop; she realized that as Supreme

Head she did not fit into a Calvinist Church. To the Catholics Calvinism was anathema.

This complicated problem was resolved in 1565 when the whole question of the religious and secular situation in the Islands, especially in Guernsey, came before the Council. The ground had been prepared by Helier de Carteret of Jersey, who crossed to England to put the case for the Islands' Synod. He pleaded the close link with Huguenot Normandy, and his fear that, if the Huguenot ministers were forbidden to use their own form of service, they would leave and the Islands would be left without pastors.

The Council was further influenced by the activities of the Guernsey Catholic jurats, to whose number Gosselin had been re-elected, against the wishes of the Governor. Three of them were known to have led an anti-Huguenot riot in St. Peter Port, 'they passed raging and crying along the streets, "Where be these Huguenotes? We will have their hartes upon the points of our swords."' Another jurat, Peter le Pelley, was known to be in correspondence with the Governor of Brittany.

Cecil's decision was also swayed by the views of Adrian Saravia, the very able Flemish refugee scholar, who had been appointed the first headmaster of Elizabeth College. He criticized the dangerous situation in the island in no uncertain terms.

In August 1565 the Council acted. The seven Guernsey jurats were dismissed from office and three of them were imprisoned in the Marshalsea. New Protestant jurats were elected and the offending jurats were pardoned on condition that they paid a fine of £1,000. This small revolution in Guernsey secured a strong Protestant Government.

At the same time the Queen and her Council recognized that the real choice in the Islands was between Calvinism and Roman Catholicism. They sanctioned the two Consistories of St. Helier and St. Peter Port, though they tried to compromise by ordering the country parishes to follow the Anglican service. They also appointed a Dean for Guernsey, whose sphere was extended to include Jersey, Chausey, Alderney and Sark. Yet the Dean, After, was himself an English Calvinist, and the spread of Calvinism was too urgent to be checked by Elizabeth's rules.

Very soon the Calvinist system and discipline were firmly established throughout the Islands, especially as more able and dedicated recruits arrived from France after 1568, the year when by the Edict of St. Maur the French Government banished all Huguenot ministers and forbade all Protestant worship on pain of death.

One of the most influential Huguenot exiles was Cosmé Brevint. He was brought over to Sark as minister of the Temple there for the new community which Helier de Carteret had established. De Carteret, the Seigneur of St. Ouen's, had feared that the uninhabited island might again become a base for a French or pirate force. In 1563 he had therefore obtained permission from the Guernsey Governor and the English Commissioners to take possession and colonize it.

He had taken his wife Margaret with him, relying on her 'grand courage and bon vouloir', and had set about reclaiming the wilderness of furze and briers that the island had become. It was a daunting task. At first Margaret had to live in the little ruined chapel of St. Magloire. All the stores, implements and animals had to be ferried across from Jersey and landed at the difficult l'Eperquerie steps.

To help him, de Carteret brought over settlers, mostly from St. Ouen's, but a few from Guernsey, and starting with a clearing round Le Manoir, they extended the settlement down the ridge of the island from north to south. In 1565 he crossed to London for an interview with Queen Elizabeth, and she was so impressed with his work that she presented the island as a fief to him (and to his heirs) on payment of forty pounds sterling and fifty shillings annual rent, on condition that he caused the island to be inhabited by '40 men at least, our subjects'. She gave generously, for in the letters patent her grant included 'all and singular castles, fortresses, houses, buildings, structures, ruins with their fragments, lands, meadows, pastures, commons, wastes, woods, waters, water courses, ponds'. To assist the island's defence, she provided six cannon from the Tower of London.

So great was the influence of Cosmé Brevint that the fifth Channel Islands Synod was held there in 1570, only six years after the first Synod was held in Guernsey. By this date a complete Presbyterian system of church government covered all the islands except Alderney, and in 1576 a set of Calvinist articles, 'Police et discipline ecclesiastique', was adopted by the full Synod at which both Governors were present. This became part of the Islands' constitutions, and the Church and the civil authorities worked closely together to enforce it.

Under this system everyone went to church, the men and the women entering by separate doors and sitting on opposite sides. All the seats faced the pulpit, and in front of it was the Table, with benches placed round so that the people could come up in relays and sit for Communion, 'as this posture agrees best with the original institution'. The service was that of the Huguenot Prayer Book, with the congregation singing from Marot's Metrical Psalms and a sermon in the morning, and in the afternoon the catechizing of the congregation in the Calvinist Catechism, a manual with four hundred answers.

After the sermon the secular business of the parish was carried out in the Temple. There the Connétable read out the orders of the Royal Court, proclaimed the transfers of property, and issued instructions about the cutting of vraic (seaweed), the very important natural fertilizer used in all the Islands.

Following the afternoon Catechism the Parish Consistory was held, which dealt with any misdeed considered wrong under their very strict code. The elders tried to make the culprit see the error of his ways; but if he would not admit and repent, he was passed on to the Island Colloquy, and the final punishment was excommunication, 'being cut off as a septic limb from the body of Christ'. The excommunicated person could not enter the Temple, or be buried in the churchyard, and any one who had dealings with him was himself excommunicated.

This discipline was backed up by the Royal Courts, with their power of sending the offender to the dungeons in the castles. Together the Church and the Government strove by innumerable Acts to make the islanders lead godly and sober lives. There were Acts against dancing, skittle-playing, and gossiping on Sundays, Acts against swearing, Acts against absence from the quarterly Communion. There was even an Act forbidding women to go sand-eeling except in the company of their husband, father or employer.

Although this system was inspired by the highest ideals, its very strictness tended to provoke rebellion. A very human example of this was the case of Marie Robilliard, a young woman of St. Pierre du Bois, Guernsey. In 1598 she was summoned before the parish Consistory because she refused to marry Roger Langlois, to whom she was betrothed. This betrothal (fiancailles) had taken place before the Colloquy and was regarded as absolutely binding; it was the rule that marriage must follow betrothal within three months. Langlois complained: 'She will not marry me; she only wants Martel.' For two years Marie held out and at last the Colloquy gave way. She was permitted to marry Martel if they did public penance. This Marie did, standing barefoot and bareheaded in St. Peter's Church, wrapped in a penitent's winding sheet before a full congregation. It was a rare occasion for the powerful Colloquy to be defeated.

More serious was the disorder reported in 1599, which brought forth the following order—'Whereas large gangs, masked and carrying clubs, career at night from house to house committing innumerable obscenities and enormities, the connétables are ordered to arrest all night-revellers, that they may receive exemplary punishment.' Twenty years later a brazen girl, Katherine le Sauteur, was convicted of joining in night revels dressed as a man and wearing knicker-bockers. She was ordered to sit all Saturday in the market stocks with her knicker-bockers hung up beside her, and again all Sunday in the stocks in St. Peter's churchyard.

The most dangerous opposition to this stern and dedicated regime came from an anti-God movement. In a superstitious period it was not difficult for unscrupulous men and women to play on the fears and desires of some of the island people. They organized actual Devil-worship, with secret midnight meetings, a disgusting ritual and horrible parodies of the Christian Sacraments. The Royal Courts and the Calvinist officials hunted down these witches' covens with ruthless determination, and the court records of this time are full of the trials of witches, for having 'practiqué le damnable art de sorcellerie'.

Guernsey records show that from 1550, when a man was executed, to 1649, when a woman was banished, there were one hundred accused, of whom eighteen were burnt, twenty-seven were hanged, strangled and then burnt, thirty-two were banished, and two were whipped and banished. The witches were of both sexes, young and old, and from all strata of society. One, Marie Renouf, convicted in Jersey, was the granddaughter of the Rector of St. John's. Another Jersey witch was the wife of a large landowner. But many were poor deluded creatures, who, if they persisted in their practices, were condemned to suffer a terrible death, in Guernsey to be burnt alive, in Jersey to be hanged and then burnt.

The most famous case occurred in 1617, when three women, Collette Dumont, Marie Dumont, and Isabell Becquet were on trial before Amyas de Carteret, Bailiff of Guernsey, and the Royal Court. The three women were convicted of practising sorcery, and causing the deaths of many persons, destroying many cattle, and other deeds, and were ordered to be tortured first to make sure of their confession to their crimes. This was the law at the time, by which they were taken to the Tour Beauregard, and there, with their thumbs tied behind them, they were lifted upwards by an engine, thus either twisting their shoulders or tearing off their thumbs. After this torture they were to be tied to a stake, strangled and burnt until their bodies were wholly consumed; finally their ashes were to be scattered abroad.

Collette admitted she was a witch. She admitted that the Devil appeared to her as a cat or dog and persuaded her to revenge herself on her enemies and to cause the deaths of men and animals. The Devil called her and invited her to the 'Sabbath', giving her a black ointment with which she anointed her body, and then, dressing again, she was carried through the air very fast to the 'Sabbath' meeting. There she met some sixteen wizards and witches, with their familiars, cats, dogs, and hares. Though she could not recognize them, blackened and disfigured as they were, the Devil called them by name, and she remembered two, Calais and Hardy. Her testimony continued that at the 'Sabbath' they adored the Devil, who stood on his hind legs in the shape of a dog, and after dancing back to back they drank some wine, poured out for them by the Devil into a silver or pewter goblet, and finally were given a black powder to throw on any enemy, to work evil or death. Similar witness, with other strange details, was given by the other two women, and they were led away to their fate.

The Calvinists endeavoured to counter these ignorant delusions by education, encouraging the setting-up of schools in every parish, to supplement the existing ones. In Jersey two free grammar schools, serving the east and the west of the island, had been founded at the end of the fifteenth century. In Guernsey there were already parish schools in St. Peter Port (La Petite École), in St. Martin, and St. Pierre du Bois, and the new Elizabeth College was making some headway, though Saravia, disgusted by the ignorance and inertia of the islanders, had left for England in 1569. He may perhaps have felt some consolation for his unfruitful experience when he was appointed by King James to be one of the translators of the Bible. Further education was assisted by a Jersey farmer, who left a trust fund to help poor boys to go to Oxford.

After the dismissals of 1565 it was broadly true that the Queen and her Council, the Governors and the officials and States of the Islands were united on general policy. But it would have been amazing if the high-spirited and independent islanders had passed the next thirty years in a spirit of complete harmony. In Jersey, where the Poulet family, Hugh, Amyas, and Anthony, held the Governorship for three generations, there was little controversy. The Poulets were connected by marriage with the island aristocracy, and as devout Puritans had a strong influence with the Calvinist Colloquy. The only internal trouble was stirred up by Jurat de Carteret, jealous of the Poulets' power. He referred to Amyas as 'Gaoler of the Castle', and engaged in a long and costly legal case against him. The chief external enemy was Spain. The Armada passed north of the Islands, though the beacon in Alderney, Macaulay's 'Aurigny's isle', flashed on the news. But Anthony Poulet decided that the defences must be strengthened. He pinned his faith in the new fortress off St. Helier, and within six years it was completed, with keep and guns and garrison. To it Sir Walter Raleigh, the Governor from 1600 to 1603, gave the name Fort Isabella Bellissima, as a tribute to his ageing mistress. His less erudite successors anglicized the name as Elizabeth Castle.

The Governorship of Guernsey was recognized to be an important and difficult post, and it was clear that the Chamberlains, father and son, were not effective or reliable enough. In 1570 Sir Thomas Leighton, an experienced soldier and diplomat and a strong Puritan, was appointed Governor. His first task was to improve the defences of Castle Cornet. In this, with the advice of Paul Ivy, a notable engineer, he succeeded, and by 1597 he had constructed an outer Tudor sheath round the old fortress, incorporating the latest Italian idea of polygonal bastions into the fortifications. This great work called for large sums of money, and Leighton was involved in many arguments with the islanders over his strict methods of raising it and over his insistence on their contribution of forced labour.

He clashed with the Royal Court over the neutrality privilege in 1586. He had seized four French ships, believing them to have Spanish goods on board. The Court declared his seizure invalid, and this disagreement brought the whole matter of local neutrality once more before the Council. They took the expert advice of Sir Amyas Poulet, that the privilege 'served for a common vent', and decided that on balance England gained from its continuance.

Another complaint against Leighton arose over his action against pirates. The island waters were a favourite haunt of pirates. It is known that the Killigrews operated in the area in Mary's reign, a Lulworth pirate actually seized despatches from Queen Elizabeth to the Governor, and by Leighton's time their numbers had been swelled by ships from many ports. These included the dangerous Barbary pirates, who in the eighties had captured William le Marchant, stepson of the Seigneur of Sausmarez. He was sent to the galleys and only ransomed with infinite trouble and expense in 1605. Not only did these pirates sweep the coasts, but they often lay to in St. Peter Port Roads. Leighton suspected that the islanders traded with them, and he was supported by a Commission of Inquiry over his attempt to use island seamen to drive them away. If the pirates were caught, their fate was certain, to hang in chains near St. Martin's Point at low water.

Although a staunch Puritan, Leighton clashed too with the ministers. In effect they recognized no superior earthly power, so when the Bishop of Winchester appointed as the Queen's Procureur Louis de Vic, 'a very honest and sufficient man and the best servant to her Majesty that ever I found in the isle,' to deal with wills and other ecclesiastical business, they denied his authority and defied for a time both the Bishop and Governor Leighton. The Council supported the Bishop and the Governor, the chief opponents among the ministers, including Nicholas Baudouin, the first Huguenot preacher, were sent away from Guernsey, and a few years later de Vic was appointed bailiff.

During his tenure of office Leighton was called on to deal with another difficult situation, in Alderney. The island had been left defenceless in Mary's reign, and had been pillaged by a French raider from Cherbourg. A second raid in 1559 was thwarted by the Guernsey Governor, Sir Leonard Chamberlain, who obtained from Elizabeth a grant of the island for his second son, George. This son was an ardent Catholic, who after Elizabeth's excommunication fled to Flanders to organize Catholic plots. However, in 1584, the third son, John, managed to secure a grant of the island, on the same terms as Helier de Carteret had been granted Sark. But Alderney already had a settled population of seven hundred, and they did not take kindly to Chamberlain's ambition to develop it. Great unrest followed, and Leighton was ordered to intervene. He, and Elizabeth's Council, were anxious that Alderney should be strongly defended and the Islanders contented, and his Ordinances, defining the rights of the Lord of the Manor and of the People, aimed to secure this. In 1591 the island became the possession of the Earl of Essex, for £1,000, but he granted a lease to yet another Chamberlain son. All the Chamberlains discouraged the Presbyterian religion, and the main substance of an island complaint against this one was that he had failed to pay a minister for sixteen years and had seized the tithes and parsonage house. The exposed position of the island, its struggling Consistory and its Catholic 'owners' caused the Guernseymen to watch it anxiously for the next forty years.

During this period, in comparison with the English, the islanders were poor. It is true that the seigneurs and the richer farming families were gradually able to live more comfortable lives. They started building solid stone houses, of two rooms at first, open to the roof; later an upstairs room, or solar, was constructed in the loft, to which the master and mistress climbed by stairs either inside or outside the house. A feature of these houses was, and still is, the round-arched doorway, of one order or layer only in Jersey, and of two, the lower recessed from the upper, in Guernsey. In these houses living was very simple; a permanent fixture was the 'green bed', or *lit d'fouaile*, on which the sleepers rested wrapped in a quilted mantle. The other fixture was the great house-table, built up by a joiner inside the living-room.

On the farms oxen did all the heavy work, ploughing the land for the crops of corn and parsnips. Cattle were few, and horses even scarcer; the chief stock was sheep, flocks of which could wander over the winter pastures by the right of common, *banaon*. They provided the owner with most of his meat, and with wool and hides for his clothes and footwear. As the richer men carefully added small field to small field, and enclosed more furze brakes and waste lands, apple orchards were planted, and cider-making became a minor industry.

The leading families, closely connected by marriage and very conscious of their rank and precedence, formed an island nobility. Many of them held office as jurats, and, as their favourite sports were hawking and falconry after the red-legged partridge, the laws against poaching were very strict. But they were not just sporting squires; many were proud of their gardens—at Trinity Manor there were peacocks and tulips, still a rarity in western Europe. A number were Oxford graduates, and records of the contents of their libraries show that some were men of wide reading and cultured tastes.

More humble, but the backbone of the island populations, were the peasant farmers, who with their families farmed their own small-holdings and were almost entirely self-supporting. The farmer gathered vraic free to manure his fields and to use on the living-room fire. He caught fish in his own boat, and extracted oil from the conger livers for his lamps. If he needed to buy anything, he took eggs or butter to market and traded for it. The little money that came his way he got from the sale of surplus corn in Normandy.

There were a few artisans, craftsmen, whose wages were firmly controlled by court orders, but the rest of the population were Les Pauvres, the poor landless and often unemployed people. Their life, if healthy, was primitive indeed; a hovel, perhaps a patch of furze on which a goat or two could browse, and whatever they could pick up in their precarious existence. Perhaps a few days' hire as a labourer, perhaps some rock-fishing, perhaps service as a seaman. A little was done for them by Church charity and parish assistance, but visitors were shocked by the number of beggars. Peter Heylyn, a college don, who came to Guernsey in the retinue of Lord Danby, the Governor, in 1628, wrote: 'Children were continually crying alms of every stranger.'

During the sixteenth century, in less dangerous times, the population of the Islands steadily increased, and yet, with the decline in the demand for salted local conger and mackerel, both from England and France, the means of earning a living decreased. No one could make a fortune out of island farming, and the more go-ahead families, with some resources, managed to branch out into overseas trade, as ship-masters, shipowners or merchants. A proclamation survives from 1459, in which Henry IV of Castile grants a safe-conduct to Thomas de Sausmarez, John Dousson, Thomas Henry and William Esstur, to come and go for trade between England and France, and orders all Spaniards to observe it.

For other islanders two new industries supplied some kind of livelihood. The more important one was the knitting of woollen goods, stockings, waistcoats and gloves. It is not known when this industry started, but by 1470 Thomas de Havilland of Guernsey had a royal grant to import wool and cloth from England, and to re-export it to Normandy and Spain. About 1500 another Guernseyman, John Bonamy, was importing raw wool and cotton yarn in his ship, *La Pitié*, and re-exporting it as knitted and woven goods, stockings and 'guernseys'. By the middle of the century the trade had made such headway that Queen Mary Tudor was happy to accept four waistcoats, four pairs of sleeves and four pairs of hose, all Guernsey knitted. Another Mary, Queen of Scots, had in her wardrobe three pairs of worsted hose, and six pairs of gloves of Guernsey manufacture. At first it was the women of Guernsey and Jersey who knitted, all the time, even secretly on Sundays. But soon the men too found that knitting was profitable. The authorities were nervous lest this cottage industry should draw them away from work on the land, but they organized it efficiently, appointing inspectors, confiscating all stockings of inferior quality, and petitioning the English Government for licences to import larger quantities of wool. The export business, to England, to France, and in the seventeenth century to America, boomed.

The second industry was the Newfoundland fishing trade. The original discovery by John Cabot had been largely exploited by fishing fleets from Brittany, Portugal and Spain; in this the port of St. Malo was a pioneer, and young Jerseymen often went as crew members on the Breton boats. Gradually Jersey boats took up this trade on their own account, and by 1590 hundreds of Jerseymen were sailing their small boats across the Atlantic, to return with their catches in the autumn before the autumn ploughing became due in their fields. In his notebook, Élie Brevint, the minister of Sark in 1620, recorded his contemporary account of the life. 'To Newfoundland they carry from here planks and nails to make boats for the fishery. The wood which they find there provides masts and oars. They must also have stages, to work on the fish and dispose of the offal. These stages are in the form of huts and little wooden houses, covered to keep out the rain. There they unload and store their salt and liquor and the fish they have in hand. The ship which arrives first in a harbour is the admiral of the year. The master allots and measures for each of the ships the length which it will have of shingle, sand or grass, for the purpose of spreading and drying the fish during the fishery.'

The Jerseymen went out to fish, and to trade, and later

as a natural development to settle. Today Nicolle, de Quetteville, Janvrin, Falla, le Feuvre and le Cocq are household names there, and areas in Newfoundland are named after their origins, St. Johns, Petty Harbour after Petty Port, Boulis Bay after Bouley Bay.

The only immediate effect of the accession of King James I was the replacement of Sir Walter Raleigh as Governor of Jersey by Sir John Peyton, a veteran soldier. He had been Lieutenant of the Tower, and apparently was on the look-out for a less difficult and invidious post. But he did not find one, for two interrelated conflicts which had simmered during Elizabeth's reign, gradually reached boiling point. The first conflict to come into the open was over the relative position of the Governor and the bailiffs and jurats of the Islands. Strong parties on both islands wanted the Governor's powers to be restricted and that 'the ancient use and authority for assembling the States for ordering the principal affairs of the island' might be re-established. Both Peyton and Leighton recognized that this was a movement towards basic constitutional change, towards a form of popular government, and resisted tooth and nail. In June 1606 deputies from both islands met in St. Peter Port and agreed to present a set of proposals jointly to the King. The result was a Commission of Inquiry in the next year, consisting of two English lawyers, with Jean Herault as the local expert. Herault was a Jerseyman of good family and a very able, honest and far-sighted man; but he had a hot temper, and his early struggles had made him intolerant of opposition. He had great influence with the Commission, the general effect of whose findings was to recognize that the bailiffs and jurats had co-equal authority with the Governors.

The second conflict broke out in Jersey. Peyton was a strong anti-Calvinist, and was determined to bring in the authority of the Anglican Church, and incidentally to exercise his claim to appoint to vacant livings. After the Hampton Court Conference and King James's famous dictum: 'No Bishop, No King.' Peyton and the Council in England were in agreement. But they had to move cautiously. Peyton was helped by a reaction amongst the laymen against the rigid Presbyterian discipline, and he did his best to undermine the authority of the Church courts. Then in 1613 he struck. Acting within his rights he appointed as rector of St. Peter's, Elie Messervy, a Jerseyman, an Oxford graduate, who had been episcopally ordained. The colloquy refused to recognize his ordination or to accept him unless he subscribed to their Discipline. This was defiance and the Council sent letters to both islands saying that it was the King's intention to establish religious uniformity in his dominions as opportunity offered. The English Government's attitude was now clear; but they were still cautious. Messervy was admitted to his benefice, but for the moment no basic changes were made.

In 1615 the constitutional conflict came to the front again. Jean Herault was appointed Bailiff of Jersey. He had evolved the theory that historically the office of bailiff was superior to that of Governor; he snubbed and thwarted Governor Peyton at every turn, and referred to him as 'Muster-master and Captain of the Troops'. The controversy raged fiercely for two years, and then yet another Commission was sent over to try to settle the two thorny questions, how to graft the Anglican system on to a proud Huguenot Church, and how to reconcile the conflicting claims of the two representatives of the Crown.

To settle the religious question the Commissioners recommended the appointment of a Dean—a position that had been in vitual abeyance since the days of Dean After. After violent argument and considerable wire-pulling, Bandinel, an Italian Protestant, Rector of St. Brelades, was appointed, and his duty was to enforce the Anglican system. As he had been one of the four religious leaders originally chosen for a deputation to London to defend Calvinism, the island Calvinists felt he was a traitor. Further he was not a Jerseyman. Years later the de Carterets referred to him as 'one Bandinel, an alien'. The Calvinists conducted a stubborn rearguard action, but Bandinel was an able and courageous man; by 1623 he had succeeded, with the full support of the Governor, the Council and the King, in imposing the Anglican form of worship and Church government on Jersey, even if many only paid lip-service to it.

Over the struggle between the Bailiff and the Governor, the Commissioners found very largely in Jean Herault's favour, and Governor Peyton was admonished for the poor state of the island defences. However, Herault then clashed with the new Dean over the election of churchwardens. When he forbade their being sworn in by the new Ecclesiastical Courts, he defied the King's instructions. He was summoned to the Council to explain, but he spoke up so boldly in reply to the Lord Chancellor, Bacon, that he found himself for a short period in the Marshalsea Prison. At last he secured a public hearing of the charges against him, and was restored to his office of bailiff by King James. His return to Jersey was almost a triumph, and, though he died in 1626, still arguing about moneys due to him, this touchy, pompous little man had fought a good fight. He had secured that the island governments should not be overriden by the military Governors sent over to them from England.

In Guernsey the situation developed very differently. By good fortune the new Governor, Lord Carew, was an absentee, and his lieutenant, Amyas de Carteret, who also held the office of bailiff, was a strong Presbyterian. Thus the ministers and the laity presented a solid and unyielding opposition to the wishes of the King and Council. Their able advocate, de la Marche, had a successful interview with King James, who agreed that the existing state of church affairs should continue. A further factor was the necessity to keep the loyalty of the islanders, now that the King's favourite, Buckingham, was in control of the British Government, and war with Spain, and later with France, was in the offing.

These wars, especially the war with France, in which Buckingham went to the Isle de Rhé off La Rochelle, to ally his mutinous troops with the Huguenots, made the position of the Islands very serious. The French Government under Cardinal Richelieu forbade all trade with them, and sent Commissioners to their own sea-ports to enforce the proclamation. On the English side a guardship from Portsmouth was sent to Jersey, and seized a French smuggler. This stopped the contraband trade. Sir Philippe de Carteret, the new bailiff, wryly remarked 'having had commission to protect the Islands, he hath almost undone us'.

There was also fear of invasion and a desperate effort was made to improve the defences. In Jersey de Carteret, who dominated Governor Peyton, was deeply concerned in this. He was personally bringing back from England money, troops and stores for the castles when he was captured by Spanish privateers from Dunkirk and was only released on the payment of a crippling ransom. Lord Danby, the Guernsey Governor, was made responsible for the defence of both islands, and by his prestige and tact secured that there was the minimum friction between the garrisons and the islanders. By 1630 peace was signed with both countries and the Islands settled back for a period of calm. On the three fronts, foreign danger, constitutional struggle, and religious differences, it appeared that a critical phase had passed.

Chapter 7

The Civil Wars

IN 1630 it happened that both Guernsey and Jersey had leading courtiers as Governors, Lord Danby for Guernsey and Sir Thomas Jermyn, who succeeded old Governor Peyton, for Jersey. After a year or so Jermyn appointed as his lieutenant the bailiff, Sir Philippe de Carteret, who lived in state in Mont Orgueil Castle with his wife and eleven children. There he maintained a little court, welcoming distinguished guests; on one occasion five Portuguese princesses on their way to Holland, on another the Queen of England's half-brother, the Duc de Vendome. He was in flight from France, charged with trying to bewitch Richelieu. The most extraordinary visitor was William Prynne, the author of *Histriomastix,* who for his alleged attack on the Queen's acting had had his ears cropped and the letters S.L. (seditious libeller) branded on his cheeks, and had now been sent to the castle as a political prisoner for attacking Archbishop Laud's bench of bishops. Prynne was well treated by the kindly de Carteret, who allowed him considerable freedom inside the castle. There he passed his time in writing verses and in making healing plasters which were sold throughout the island.

De Carteret's firm control ensured a number of years of peace and efficient government, but there were strong currents of unrest beneath the surface. He had reserved most of the important posts for his own clan, and had secured the King's promise that he should be succeeded as bailiff by his brother Élie, and that Élie should be succeeded by his brother George.

This prospect of a long period of de Carteret domination did not please other Jersey families, notably the Lemprières and the Dumaresqs; nor did de Carteret's favour with Archbishop Laud, by whose influence he secured an endowment at Oxford to train Jerseymen as Anglican clergy. Gradually the opposition consolidated into a party, known locally as *Les Refractaires*, to whom was added a powerful recruit in Bandinel, the Dean of Jersey. He had quarrelled with the Lieutenant-Governor over the right to church tithes.

This clash caused the case to be referred to Westminster, and there went de Carteret to deal with this challenge to his authority as Lieutenant-Governor and bailiff. He could not have chosen a more difficult time. The Scottish Commissioners and their soldiers were in control of the North of England, the Long Parliament under the expert handling of Pym was starting on its revolutionary course, and Strafford and Laud were under arrest. De Carteret's case was not dealt with, and his Jersey enemies, hopeful of the Long Parliament, pursued him with a petition and complaint of twenty-one charges, stating that 'he bears sundry offices incompatible in one person'.

They relied on William Prynne, who had been released and was the idol of the Londoners, to see that the petition was presented. But Prynne had not forgotten de Carteret's kindness to him, and he saw to it that the petition was suppressed. Then a report came in that there were forty thousand French troops in St. Malo. At this time the Parliamentarians saw the hand of the Queen everywhere, behind the Catholicism of the bishops, behind the army plots in York, and now in a threat to invade the Islands. De Carteret was released from attendance on Parliament and sent back to his post in Jersey.

There, as the split between the two sides in England grew wider and both prepared for war in 1642, Sir Philippe tried to carry on his government with loyalty to the King but also to keep the island out of the impending struggle. This reasonable plan of neutrality was wrecked by two developments. First his island opponents, led by the Dean and including five of the jurats, formed themselves into a definite party, and they were in close touch with kindred spirits on the Puritan side in England. Secondly, his nephew, George de Carteret, later generally known as George Carteret, was a forceful and experienced officer in the Royal Navy. Although almost all the ships had deserted the King and had put themselves cheerfully under the orders of Parliament's admiral, the Earl of Warwick, de Carteret had sailed his ship to St. Malo. From there he was running arms and munitions to the Royalists in the West Country and was preying on ships bound for London. In January 1643 he supplemented his supplies of ammunition by sailing in and commandeering stocks from Elizabeth Castle. Sir Philippe did nothing to check this action, the first open breach of the island's neutrality, and his opponents had the opening they were looking for.

Orders arrived from Parliament that Michel Lemprière and Henri Dumaresq, the leaders of the pro-Parliament Committee, should arrest Sir Philippe and take over the island on behalf of Parliament. A dramatic scene took place in the States, where Sir Philippe faced his accusers and denied their authority. He countered Parliament's orders by producing a letter from Charles commanding his subjects to obey his deputy, and he stuck stoutly to his constitutional argument, 'This island has nothing to do with Parliament, but only with the King in Council': an argument which was legally correct but not acceptable to his revolutionary opponents. They had learnt from Pym's successful use of the London mob, and had taken their precautions. They had called out the militiamen of St. Saviour's and St. Clement's, and before the threat of violence Sir Philippe was forced to withdraw to Elizabeth Castle while his wife remained safe in Mont Orgueil. Encouraged by the support of his own group,

Les Bien Affectionés, he still tried to negotiate, but at last on 1st May, he turned the castle guns on some Parliamentary ships which were pursuing a Royalist frigate. The Civil War in Jersey had begun.

The leaders of the Parliamentary Committee in Guernsey had received the same orders from Parliament, to arrest the Lieutenant-Governor and to hold the island for Parliament and for the Parliamentary Governor the Earl of Warwick. There the situation had developed with significant differences. In the first instance the Earl of Danby had appointed as his lieutenant his brother-in-law, Sir Peter Osborne. This Osborne, of an old Essex landed family, who held the hereditary office of Treasurer's Remembrancer in the Exchequer of James I, had taken up his post in 1621. He, an Englishman, was a devoted and obstinate servant of the House of Stuart. Through the years, though he governed the island justly and efficiently, he did little to earn the liking or the affections of the islanders. In fact he seems to have been very aloof, and to have spent most of his time living in solitary state in his official residence in Castle Cornet. There is no evidence that his wife and family shared his life on the rocky fortress. The nearest they appear to have been to him was later, at the beginning of the castle seige, when his wife and his famous daughter, Dorothy, the delightful letter-writer, did their best to victual the castle from their retreat in St. Malo.

Another reason for Sir Peter's lack of accord with the islanders must have been that to him, a devout Anglican, their sturdy Presbyterianism, with its touch of Republicanism, was not congenial. During the period before the Civil War, King James's decision that on political grounds the island's Presbyterian system of Church government should not be tampered with was allowed to stand. Yet the islanders knew of the increasing influence of Archbishop Laud in the English Government, and they must have learnt of his declared intention to make them conform. Laud had actually selected a person to make a visitation of the island, and he had won round Charles the First to the view that 'as great if not greater care of conformity ought to be had of this island as of Jersey'. Further he brought great pressure to bear on Lord Danby to support him. This, fortunately for the Presbyterians, the Governor resisted, arguing the foolishness of such action. Danby's resistance, in 1637, postponed direct action by the logical Archbishop, who then found himself involved in the consequences of similar action in Scotland, the Prayer Book Riots, and he and his King had no time for Guernsey.

There were other reasons for the unpopularity of Charles and his Government. A royal decree of 1628 had stifled a new industry which some of the more enterprising islanders had started, that of tobacco-growing. The official reason was the fear that it would destroy the King's Customs and would harm the plantations in Virginia. He was unpopular, too, with the merchants and seamen, for with the run-down of the Royal Navy the seas were now more dangerous, and he had done nothing to help ransom prisoners captured by pirates. Another source of anger was his failure to provide money for the garrison; Castle Cornet was a royal fortress and this payment was the King's liability, and yet the islanders were forced to raise large sums to keep it in good repair.

All these points, religious, constitutional, financial and defensive tended to unite the islanders, especially the merchants, townsmen and seamen, in opposition to the King, and to make them look sympathetically on the resistance being developed by the Parliamentarians in England. Unlike Jersey, there was no leading family, of outstanding wealth and estates, to uphold the King's cause and to stand for the traditional loyalties.

There were very few Royalists in Guernsey. Only Henry de Vic, Charles's French secretary, who lived away from the island for most of his life, Peter Priaulx, Seigneur of Fief le Comte, and members of the Andros family, descendants of an English official named Andrews, who had come to the island in Tudor times.

Against them were ranged the most influential families. The leader, and typical of them, was Pierre de Beauvoir, who combined the position of landowner with that of merchant. He held the estate of Les Granges and owned houses in the High Street, and he had trading connections with Spain, Brittany and Le Hague, exchanging wool, silk and velvet goods for French linens and laces, brandy and gloves and Spanish wines. He was linked by marriage with important Huguenot families in St. Malo and the West Country, and in Guernsey with the Careys. Pierre Carey was his brother-in-law, and these two, with James de Havilland, were the leaders of the twelve jurats appointed as Parliamentary Commissioners in March 1643, with orders to arrest Osborne and hold the island for Parliament. The Royalist bailiff, de Quetteville, was arrested for failing to take action when he was notified that George Carteret the sailor had reached Castle Cornet seeking arms and ammunition, and Pierre de Beauvoir was appointed President of the Island Parliamentary Government.

Naturally Sir Peter Osborne refused to recognize what was to him an illegal and revolutionary régime, and replied to de Beauvoir's orders, 'No summons, by virtue of what power soever, hath command here.' He shut himself and a small garrison up in Castle Cornet and trained and fired his guns into the town. Some colour was lent to the suspicions against de Quetteville, for, though his brewhouse was the nearest building to the castle, it was never hit.

In his cramped rocky fortress Osborne held out for nearly three years, he and his garrison suffering great privations, and being supplied with great difficulty with ammunition and provisions from Jersey after the Royalists under George Carteret had regained control there, St. Malo and Cornwall. His garrison seems to have stood by him loyally; only once is there a record of any trouble. Osborne had struck one of his gunners, who were key men, with the flat of his sword. The garrison mutinied and shut him up in his house, with two cannon pointing at the door. His main difficulty was in his dealings with Sir George Carteret in Jersey, who sent him in supplies unwillingly and at irregular intervals, and was mean enough to demand payment for these stores. At last Carteret's hostility and influence led to the replacement of Osborne by Sir Bernard Wake, and on Wake's disappearance in 1649 the third commander of the royal stronghold was a Colonel Burgess.

To the islanders this great fortress, dominating their town and harbour, was a grave menace. At any time balls from the castle guns could crash into the streets and houses at the southern end of the town. Balls whistled over the Plaiderie, the Court House, to embed themselves in the hill beyond. No one was safe in the area. Ironically Peter Priaulx, who had been involved in a plot to seize Jerbourg Castle for the King, and after escaping had later been allowed to return to the island, was killed by a castle cannon-ball as he walked down the Pollet in St. Peter Port.

Not only did the castle guns terrorize and damage the town, they dominated the harbour and roadstead, too, seriously interrupting the trading activities of the islanders and checking the expeditions of the fishing boats. Some use was made of the haven at St. Sampson's, but it was no replacement for the great deep roadstead.

This situation imposed a heavy responsibility on the island leaders. The Parliamentary Lieutenant-Governor was a Russell, a weak man who angered the islanders by imposing taxes and using troops to collect them. But Pierre de Beauvoir as Bailiff and Pierre Carey as Lieutenant-Bailiff made a strong team, capable of dealing with any disaffection that might arise as the islanders grew disillusioned with the war.

Yet their cause nearly suffered disaster early in the struggle. A Captain Bowden, who held a Parliamentary commission, had sailed his ship, *The George*, from Guernsey to Dartmouth. There he was persuaded by Prince Maurice to change sides, and was sent back to Guernsey to try to seize the persons of Russell and de Beauvoir, Carey and de

Havilland. Anchoring in the harbour, he persuaded the three jurats to come on board for a conference. He held them prisoner and sailed off for Jersey, in the hope of succeeding with a similar trick there. But Russell's suspicions had been aroused; not only had he avoided the trap, but he had also sent off a boat quickly to Jersey to warn the Parliamentary leaders there. Back to Guernsey sailed Bowden and off the castle he was forced by Osborne's soldiers to hand over the three men. They were brought before the Royalist Governor, who stared at them in stony silence, and then condemned them to the lowest dungeon. As Pierre Carey recorded in his diary, 'In one of the deepest dungeons under the lowest ditch, a place so subterranean and humid that our hair became wet, and from thence we were unable to see light but through the keyhole.' After some weeks they were moved to an upper dungeon, where they managed to get hold of some cotton. Twisting it into ropes, for the three stages of their escape, they got away through a window to the rocks below. Fired at from the castle, they scrambled away across the rocks at low tide, and were received with a rapturous welcome as they returned safely to the town.

Stiffened by their narrow escape these men led the island throughout the wars, backed at all times by the authority and encouragement of the Governor, the Earl of Warwick. He supported their application for a licence to continue the export of wool from England to Guernsey, to supply the knitting industry. This was hard hit, not only by the castle blockade, but also because the Queen Regent of France forbade any trade from North-west France unless the trader had a pass signed by the Royalist Governor.

To deal with the threat from the castle, and a little later from Jersey, Warwick had arms and supplies of powder sent over from the Tower of London, demi-cannon, four culverins, and three hundred muskets.

The leaders did not forget the other islands. There was no need to take action over Herm and Jethou. As Dr. Heylyn reported, 'Two of them (i.e. isles) lie along betwixt it and Serke, viz. Arme and Jethow, whereof this last serveth only as a parke unto the governor, and hath in it a few fallow deer and good plenty of coneys. The other of them is well near three miles in circuit, a solitary dwelling of canons regular, and afterwards of some fryers of the order of St. Francis, but now only inhabited by pheasants.' To Alderney was sent an officer, Pierre Le Febure, with orders to expel all Papists and to organize the militia and defences to resist any attack by the Jersey Royalists. Sark, too, was brought under control. A small Parliamentary garrison was established, which was popular with the islanders. There was some friction with the seigneur, Philippe II de Carteret, and eventually he was driven out. The one Jersey raid on Sark, when a Captain Chamberlain and thirty men got ashore, ended ignominiously with the capture of the whole party.

In Jersey meanwhile events did not run so smoothly for the Parliamentarians. They had some initial success, as a raid by Royalist hotheads from Elizabeth Castle, supported by the castle guns, was checked by musket fire from the townspeople, and the Cavaliers were forced to gallop back in case the rising tide cut them off. By August too Sir Philippe was dead, struck down by an epidemic in the castle and giving his last orders, 'That they should not bury his body till the King had overcome his enemies.'

But the Parliamentarians underestimated the difficulties in Jersey. An able cavalry officer, Lydcot, was sent to them as Lieutenant-Governor, to bring his expert knowledge to bear on the problems of capturing the two castles, Elizabeth and Mont Orgueil. He did manage to tighten up the siege sufficiently for the Royalist commander only to be able to learn the news from England from a code of signals conveyed by the number of sheets hung out on his wife's washing-line at St. Aubin's, across the bay from Elizabeth Castle. Yet, relying on the Jersey militia, Lydcot came over with no troops and only six officers. The Jerseymen became disheartened. With their farms to look after, they could not give their whole time to the siege, and they realized how impossible was their task when the castles could be supplied so easily from the sea.

Disagreement arose between Lydcot and Lemprière, the bailiff, over the usual bone of contention between Governors and Island authorities, the status of the States. There was also religious discord. The majority of Jersey's leaders were Presbyterians, and to these men Lydcot's Independent religious views were as hateful as those of an Episcopalian. Other Jersey leaders had turned to Anabaptism, so that to the orthodox it seemed as if religious anarchy was on the way.

The Royalists scented this disaffection when the States tried to open up negotiations with Sir Philippe's widow in Mont Orgueil, and it gave the opening for which George Carteret had been waiting.

He had been appointed lieutenant for the Royalist Governor Jermyn and bailiff, and collecting a scratch force of English, Irish, Scots and French in St. Malo, he made a safe landing at Mont Orgueil on Sunday, 19th November 1643. There was little resistance from the militia, and the Parliamentary Committee quickly realized that their position was hopeless. Some forty people got away to Guernsey and within three days Carteret had occupied the town.

He quickly secured the submission of the States, and tried to bring home the situation to the islanders by summoning the men in batches of ten to swear loyalty to the King. However the average Jerseyman's attitude was negative, passive, and Carteret failed completely to raise a force of volunteers to set out to reduce Guernsey, nor did he succeed any better in raising money from them for the Royalist cause.

For revenue he had to rely on privateering. Starting with a single swift galley, he gradually added to his fleet, and soon had built up a big enterprise. At first he was, strictly speaking, a pirate, but after six months he was appointed Vice-Admiral of Jersey, so that the cargoes seized by his ships—hats, snuff, paving-stones, oranges, lemons, and stockings—could be brought to his Vice-Admiral's Court, there declared 'a good and lawful prize' and then be sold in Fécamp.

Some of Carteret's opponents in Jersey were stubborn. Held prisoner in the dungeons of Mont Orgueil, they were tried by a Royalist Commission. Among them were Jurat Bisson, who refused to retract the orders of the Parliament Commission; and the Royalist Rector of St. Ouen's, Etienne la Cloche, who had thundered against Carteret from his pulpit, accusing him of turning Jersey into a pirates' lair. The oldest opponent of the Carteret interest, Dean Bandinel, tried to escape down a rope to the rocks below the castle, but crashed to his death when the rope broke. This resistance, in one form or another, nonplussed the Royalists, and they were further restrained by the threat of the English Parliament to execute three prisoners for every death caused by Carteret. So that the best solution they could devise was to fine the recalcitrants heavily and to confiscate the property of those who had escaped.

Even though Carteret declared in a manifesto 'Party squabbles in the English Parliament are no concern of ours. Let us remain true to our Duke and to our Constitution,' there was little popular loyalty to Carteret and to the Royalist cause until April 1646. Then a great deal of excitement and some enthusiasm was caused by the arrival of the fifteen-year-old Charles, Prince of Wales, whom Fairfax had driven out of the West of England. He arrived with a motley collection of followers—high-minded Loyalists, scallywags, young pages, old alcoholic lords, and ladies of varied respectability. Lodgings had to be found for most of them in the town, but Charles stayed in Elizabeth Castle. He himself charmed the islanders—'C'etoit un Prince grandement benin,' wrote Chevalier, the Royalist Vingtenier of St. Helier—as he performed official functions, attending service in the Town Church and reviewing the island militia.

His advisers, among whom were men of calibre, the

Lords Capel, Hopton and Colepepper, and Sir Edward Hyde, had two great worries, lack of money and the intrigues of the Prince's French Catholic mother, Henrietta Maria. Hyde did his best to counteract her efforts to lure the boy away to France, into the power of Cardinal Mazarin. On 25th June, however, Charles sailed away with his Court, leaving his best men behind, among them Hyde, who passed his time writing a large part of his *History of the Rebellion*.

Very soon the Royalist Court in Paris was bankrupt and the staunch Loyalists in Jersey were much disturbed by a strong rumour that negotiations were on foot through Jermyn to sell the Channel Isles to France for 200,000 pistoles. Carteret and the others were ready to appeal for help to the English Parliament as 'it would be an irreparable dishonour to the English Crown'. However the danger passed, possibly because Cardinal Mazarin would not agree to pay such a price, more probably because no one could raise a force to reduce Parliamentary Guernsey.

The Jersey Loyalists faced threats from England too, where Bailiff Lemprière, Dumaresq and others were assisting the Government and trying to stir it to recover Jersey. Nothing was done until the King had been captured in January 1647, and then Parliament was prepared to reduce the Royalist pockets of resistance. Carteret and his associates were anxious, as they knew well that the majority of the islanders would side with an invading Parliamentary army. But their luck held. The quarrel broke out between the New Model Army and the Parliament, and in the turmoil of the ensuing Second Civil War Jersey was forgotten. 'God brake their plans and saved us,' said Chevalier.

This respite enabled the islanders to carry on their daily lives almost normally. The States met fortnightly. The Royal Court sat weekly. The farmers farmed and the fishing fleet sailed to Newfoundland. But it was an increasing struggle to make a living, now that the stocking trade had been almost brought to a standstill.

Meanwhile Sir George Carteret continued his efforts to

intervene actively in the Royalist cause. An attempt was made to get in touch with the King, now in Carisbrooke Castle, but Charles preferred to rely on his own cunning rather than Jersey help. Carteret's other plans, to invade Guernsey and to reduce Sark were foiled, the first through the jealousy of the Guernsey Governor, Wake, who refused to allow Carteret to enter Castle Cornet with more than six men. A great storm stopped his planned raid on Sark.

By January 1649 the King's futile plottings had convinced Cromwell and the army leaders that the only solution was his death, 'We will cut off his head with the Crown upon it,' and the Rump Parliament abolished the office of king as 'unnecessary, burdensome and dangerous'. True to character Carteret pursued his own course and had Charles II proclaimed in Jersey. He receive the unexpected reinforcement of a Parliamentary frigate, *The Heart*. Her crew had seized her as she lay in the Downs, and sailed her to Jersey to join his fleet. *The Heart* then sailed to Guernsey, and enticing another Parliamentary frigate away from the cover of the land batteries, took her as a prize.

In September the young King retreated from France to Jersey. A crowd of officials and courtiers came with him, all of whom had to be provided with board and lodging, and the King's financial position grew ever more desperate. This does not appear to have worried Charles. While Ormonde in Ireland and the gallant Montrose in Scotland risked their lives for him, he passed his time pleasantly enough, hunting hares, rabbits and partridges by day, and dancing in the castle by night. The island gossips were kept amused by the stories of the houses the King had visited, of the strange scenes when he touched for the King's Evil in the castle chapel, and of the rivalries and jealousies among his supporters.

At last, in February 1650, he cynically accepted what looked to be the best offer of support from the Scottish Covenanters led by Argyll, and sailed away to meet the Scottish Commissioners.

After this strange interlude life in Jersey returned to normal once more. But Carteret was shrewd enough to realize that Cromwell must try to put down those parts of the Empire which had proclaimed another government, and prepared for his inevitable attack. He enlisted more mercenaries, Poles, Swedes, and Danes, whose thieving made them very unpopular. 'Off all nations that have come to Jersey', wrote Chevalier, 'the Germans (the island name for them) are the worst thieves. The Irish are terrible plundererers, but these rogues beat them hollow.' He also welcomed pirates from all nations, to whom he issued Letters of Marque, official commissions, to prey on English shipping, an example followed by Prince Rupert in Holland. By Cromwell's Government they were all classed as 'Jersey' pirates, and the reckoning with Carteret mounted each day. In all it is estimated that privateering brought him in £60,000.

By October 1651 Colonel Heane, the Commander-in-Chief of Dorset, was ready. He embarked 2,600 men and two troops of horse, and with the escorting warships of the formidable Admiral Blake, he set sail to reduce the island. Heavy seas made the original landing by boat in St. Ouen's Bay impossible, and Heane, with Blake's support, had to make feints at various points on the coast. By the night of 22nd October Carteret's militia were soaked from a continuous downpour, hungry, tired and mutinous. Led by a party of Guernseymen the New Model Army landed safely at the southern end of St. Ouen's. By the next night only the two castles remained in Royalist hands. Mont Orgueil capitulated quickly, the garrison being disheartened by the knowledge of the 'crowning mercy' of Worcester and tempted by Heane's generous terms. Elizabeth Castle was a tougher proposition. Carteret had improved its defences and brought in large stocks of food and ammunition for its garrison of 340 men. It was effectively out of range of Heane's guns, and he was forced to send to Portsmouth for Parliament's heaviest artillery, 'cannon as big as barrels', which fired bombs containing forty pounds of powder. The third shot crashed into the chapel crypt, where the castle powder was stored, and the explosion not only destroyed most of Carteret's supplies, but demoralized the garrison. He was authorized by Charles II to get what terms he could, and after shrewd bargaining the garrison marched out on 15th December, 'ensigns flying, drums beating, matches alight at both ends, bullets in mouth'. Carteret bargained well for himself, as he was allowed to keep all his property, and he left for France. There he became a vice-admiral in the French Navy, and kept a high place in the King's favour; one reward for his loyalty was the grant in 1659 of lands in America. But the friends and supporters he left behind in Jersey had to hand over two years' income to escape confiscation of their property.

Castle Cornet was now left as the last outpost of the Royalist cause, and on 19th December Colonel Burgess and his garrison of fifty-five men surrendered, marching out with the honours of war. Burgess was granted an indemnity of £1,500, as a reward for the humane way in which he had treated some Parliamentary prisoners, taken earlier in an abortive attack.

The removal of the castle's threat to the town and to the island shipping was a great relief to the Guernseymen, but they were still kept under the firm military control of Cromwell's representative, Colonel Bingham. At the time of Charles II's proclamation as King two years before, the garrison had been increased to five companies, and the islanders groaned under the strain of providing for them. They petitioned the Lord Protector, and dared to ask that Castle Cornet should be dismantled and the island be returned to its inhabitants. This petition was rejected by General Lambert, who ironically enough was to find himself a political prisoner in the castle at the Restoration. But the control of the seas by the Protectorate's Navy, and the diminished threat to the Islands ensured that the garrison was gradually reduced to a company, and the Guernseymen were comparatively free to go about their daily business.

A similar military government was set up in Jersey under Colonel Heane. Lemprière returned from England to take over his old post as bailiff, and Carteret's officials were replaced by men who had suffered for the Commonwealth. But Heane had many problems. One was the behaviour of the troops from Guernsey, who carried off to their ships whatever they could lay hands on. A more lasting difficulty was caused by his own Parliamentary troops, the majority of whom were Independents in religion. They secularized the Presbyterian temples, destroying the pews and the table of the Town Church, and interrupting the services which the country rectors struggled manfully to carry on. Eventually, though he could not understand the French service, Heane attended the Town Church to secure some respect.

The most intractable problems arose from the claims of the returned exiles to property which they stated they had had to sell to save their lives, and from the complications of trying to assess the value of two years' income which the Royalists were liable to forfeit. Many and fierce were the arguments between Lemprière and Maret, the receiver, as they strove to reach a fair assessment.

Further uncertainty arose from a well-grounded fear that the Parliamentary Council in England might change the Island Constitution. In fact, in 1653, the Instrument of Government which appointed Cromwell to be Protector, decreed that Jersey should send one member to the House of Commons. This order was ignored. However, in the island there was no form of representative government either, as the States did not meet during the Commonwealth. Lemprière, the bailiff, struggled on almost single-handed, for he had no jurats to help him in the administration of justice or to form a quorum in the States, and as an Anabaptist he refused to allow the rectors to attend. These rectors, led by Josué de la Place of Trinity had re-established Presbyterianism and the Huguenot form of service, so that the divisions between the civil and religious leaders were profound.

Lemprière's position as bailiff was regularized by the issue of new letters patent, which replaced the old commission of Charles I and instituted him as bailiff for his Highness Oliver, Lord Protector of the Commonwealth. Yet he still had not a sufficient number of jurats to hold a properly constituted court. Another difficulty for him and for the islanders came from the character of the new commander, Colonel Gibbon. He was a truculent soldier, who despised and virtually ignored the civilian government, punishing as he wished and ruling with an iron hand. It was with his support that a Navy press gang was able to pick up fifty men from Guernsey and Jersey, although this was contrary to the charters and was firmly opposed by the Guernsey Court. Gibbon condoned the action of some of his soldiers, who used the threat of impressment for service in Jamaica to extort money from rich families. Another form of extortion which he openly engaged in was the billeting of troops at free quarters in the houses of those Royalists who could not pay their fines. If the unhappy householder complained, he learnt that he could borrow money from Gibbon's son at 30 per cent interest. To check any letters of complaint on these matters to England, he applied a personal censorship.

Unrest in Jersey grew, and it reached such a pitch in 1657 that in a jurat election two ex-Royalist were elected. The poll had to be declared void and a new election held. The only result was that the Jurat Roll now contained five of Lemprière's relatives, still not enough to produce a full court. Even the English garrison was restive; Honest John Lilburne, the leader of the radical Levellers in Cromwell's New Model Army, was a prisoner in Mont Orgueil, and his presence stirred them up.

With the collapse of the Protectorate after Cromwell's death and the restoration of the Long Parliament, the Jerseymen began to hope that they would be freed at last from Gibbon's long tyranny. He was recalled to serve in England, but he was replaced by another, a Colonel Mason, a forceful

Anabaptist, and it seemed that Red-Coat rule was clamped on them for ever.

At last, in January 1660, General Monk moved down from Scotland to intervene in the chaos into which the English republic had collapsed. He appointed Colonel Carew Raleigh as Governor of Jersey, and in April sent over his own representative, Captain Hanley. Charles's Declaration of Breda had already reassured the people, and when the news arrived on 2nd June that Charles II had entered London in triumph, the Vicomte joyfully proclaimed the King in the market-place. 'The cannons fired, muskets went off everywhere, bonfires blazed in all the parishes.' A week or two before, Lemprière and the other Commonwealth officials had slipped away quietly across the sea to Coutainville.

In Guernsey during these times of change and uncertainty there was great anxiety and little rejoicing. They had not had to endure a tyrant like Gibbon, and they had stood loyally in turn by the Long Parliament, the Presbyterians, and the Protector through all the years of war and revolution. Now their cause appeared hopeless. Relying on the Declaration of Breda and on the fact that the Convention Parliament which recalled Charles was largely Presbyterian, the Guernsey authorities made humble submission. It is true that they received a general pardon and that the new Lieutenant-Governor, Captain Darrell, was a man with island connections and one whom they respected. But they awaited the coming of the King's nominee as Governor, Lord Hatton, and the view that the King's Council would adopt towards such stubborn opponents, with apprehension.

Chapter 8

Privateering and Prosperity

AFTER his restoration Charles II and his Council stood loyally and tolerantly by the Declaration of Breda. The charters and privileges of the Islands were renewed, and a general amnesty, in the spirit of the Act of Indemnity and Oblivion, was granted to all those who in the eyes of the extreme Royalists were rebels and traitors.

The Guernseymen accepted the situation with relief and outward rejoicing. Already Charles had been proclaimed there, 'with ringing of bells, half companies of the most expert of the militia under arms, *feu de joie*, and great rejoicings. The proclamation was read before the Plaiderie, at the Grand Carrefour, before Berthelot Street, before the cage, at the church door, and on the pier,' as Peter le Roy, the French schoolmaster, recalled.

In Jersey the Royalist jurats, who had been restored to their positions, while the full quota was made up by the election of 'men of known loyalty', jibbed at their loss of revenge. They neglected to register the Act, and on the strength of this a number of Republicans had their estates confiscated. Petition after petition went to Westminster, and at last in 1669 a royal order specifically laid down that the Act applied to Jersey as well as to all the other dominions of the King.

Naturally enough Charles saw to it that political control in the Islands passed to men he felt he could rely upon. Sir George Carteret himself held a high place at the English Court, as Vice-Chamberlain and Privy Councillor, and his naval experience was rewarded with the post of Comptroller of the Navy, whereby he became a colleague of Samuel Pepys. Loans he had made to the King were repaid with manors in Cornwall and Devon, and with lands in America, in particular the province of New Jersey, to which he sent out his cousin Philippe as Governor in 1664.

The de Carteret influence in Jersey was supreme, with George's brother, Philippe, as bailiff, under the new Lieutenant-Governor, Thomas, nephew of the old courtier, Jermyn. The King endeavoured to symbolize the island's loyalty by the presentation of a silver-gilt mace, 'as proof of his royal affection towards the island of Jersey, in which he had twice been received in safety when excluded from the remainder of his dominions'. This mace is still borne before the bailiff and officials of the island on state occasions.

Control of Alderney also passed to Sir George. Aiming to reduce the power of the Guernsey Governor and Royal Court, Charles separated Alderney's government from that of the bigger island and vested it in Sir George. The new Governor appointed a Captain Ling as his deputy on the island, and an able and conscientious minister, the Reverend Picot, to carry through the religious reorganization which was laid down by the Act of Uniformity.

In spite of the amnesty, Guernsey remained the problem island. Amias Andros, of the outstanding Royalist family, was appointed Bailiff, de Quetteville, son of the man who had held office in 1640, was restored to his position of Lieutenant-Bailiff, and loyal men were placed on the Jurats' Bench to support them. But the new Governor, Lord Hatton, did not arrive in the island until 1664, and by that date the situation was tense.

The Cavalier Parliament, which Charles retained for eighteen years, had been elected on a surge of reaction and panic after the Fifth Monarchy Rising. The members were determined on two things, to maintain the power of Parliament, and to restore the full power and influence of the Anglican Church. In its first five years this Parliament passed the Clarendon Code, an outright attempt to stamp out Puritanism, and as part of this in 1662 it passed the Act of Uniformity, which was to apply to all the King's dominions.

The Guernseymen, especially the ministers and the general mass of the people, clung fiercely to their long-established Presbyterian forms of church government and service, and the battle between them and the new Dean, John de Sausmarez, was a bitter one. Backed up by a body of troops, he had to use all the powers of a forceful personality and the authority of the Royal Court to crush the opposition. Against him stood a minister, Thomas le Marchant, an able and intelligent man, as the leader of the Presbyterian party, who was only silenced by being imprisoned first in Castle Cornet, and later in the Tower of London for two years. Five other ministers lost their parishes, and on the surface the Anglican cause triumphed. But resistance continued to the Anglican form of service, to the Liturgy, to the sign of the Cross in Baptism, and to kneeling at Communion. In fact, baptismal fonts were only introduced in 1829 on the orders of the Bishop of Winchester, Dr. Sumner, the first to visit this part of his diocese since Queen Elizabeth placed the island under the See of Winchester some two hundred and fifty years before. Again, as no bishop had sailed across to hold a Confirmation service until 1818, the stubborn islanders kept to the Presbyterian forms, by which the catechumens were examined before the Consistory.

Another factor which raised doubts in the minds of the English Council was the presence in Castle Cornet as a political prisoner of General Lambert. It was feared that he might become the figure-head of a new republican movement in the island, and outside.

In this atmosphere arrived Lord Hatton to take up his residence in Castle Cornet. He quickly alienated the islanders, by referring to the castle as his palace, and by abusing all the island leaders, from the bailiff downwards, as factious robbers and thieves. Those who had led the island during the Commonwealth, de Beauvoir, Carey, and de Havilland, were promptly removed from office.

Yet it was Hatton himself, a weak and unbalanced man, who drew the islanders together. Complaint after complaint went to Westminster, of his arbitrary interference with the course of justice, and of his dishonesty, until Charles was forced to recall him. A sound and sympathetic officer, Colonel Atkins, was appointed to command the island, until Hatton's son, Christopher, the husband of Lambert's daughter Mary, should take up the Governor's position.

The other influence to unify the islanders occurred in 1666. The Dutch and English were already at war, and then Louis XIV joined in, declaring war on England. The rumour spread that he would open his campaign by an attempt to capture Jersey, and that there was a plot to use Lambert as the figure-head of revolt in Guernsey. The plot was given away by the wife of the French Marshal, Turenne. She was a Protestant, and passed on what information she had gleaned to a Jersey minister. This timely information and the good sense and leadership of Colonel Atkins rallied the Guernseymen. He was known anyway as a man who had their interests at heart; he wrote with pride in 1667, in one of the earliest references to Guernsey privateering: 'How bravelie the men of St. Martyn's have behaved themselves at sea. They have brought in a prize of 60 Ton, of Amsterdam, laden with wine, tobacco, figs and rosin.'

This external threat drew the Jerseymen together too. There the divisions were less severe, for the Anglican system had been in force before, and the Dean, Philippe le Couteur, had strong backing for the firm enforcement of the Anglican service and discipline. Clerical and lay dissentients found themselves before his Ecclesiastical Court, and no departure was allowed from the set forms of the service, translated rather amateurishly into French.

The doddering old Jermyn was replaced as Governor by a fiery little Welshman, Sir Thomas Morgan, one of Monk's right-hand men. He made great efforts to prepare the island against enemy attack. The militia was remodelled, grouped in three regiments and dressed in Coldstream red, and given intensive training. The defences of Elizabeth Castle were completed. Although the threatened invasion did not materialize and peace was soon proclaimed, Morgan's galvanic energy had another success. He undertook the building of St. Aubin's pier, which ran out three hundred feet from the fort and made the first protected harbour in the island, capable of taking the largest ships of the Newfoundland fishing fleet, and offering a safer anchorage to foreign merchant vessels.

But Governor Morgan despised the island officials and there was constant friction with the Royal Court, whose orders he ignored. On one occasion he shook his cane at a constable in court, shouting, 'By God, sirrah, I will rub your nose.' Jurats who displeased him were repaid by having troops quartered in their houses.

This failure to identify himself with the interests of the islanders led to further trouble over the Navigation Act. This laid down that no goods could be imported into the plantations in America except in English ships. As a considerable trade had grown up between Jerseymen carrying stockings from Jersey, and other Jerseymen who had settled in America and sent back cargoes of cod, rum or molasses, the Act, which Morgan enforced, caused much hardship. For the islanders could not get the Government to accept that Jersey ships were English.

Morgan died in 1679, to be succeeded by another veteran, a grizzled one-eyed soldier, who continued the running fight with the Jersey States, and with their spokesman in London, Sir Edouard de Carteret, the Vicomte or executive officer of the States. Only the King's personal intervention stopped a duel between the two in Hyde Park.

During these years the Guernseymen had had an excitement of another kind. The second Lord Hatton had taken up his post as Governor in 1670, and owing to memories of his father had received a cool reception. 'Not a gunn was

5 Castle Cornet, Guernsey, A.D. 1672

6 The end of the French attempt to take Jersey, 1779 (*by permission of the Leger Galleries*)

heard for a wellcome usually given to anybody that comes from the King.' But by his kindliness and concern for the island's prosperity he soon changed their hostility to friendship. One of his many attractive traits was his love of flowers; he cultivated the Guernsey Lily (*Nerine Sarniensis*), the origin of which was attributed locally to the fairies, but which was actually brought to the island by a sailor rescued from a Dutch ship sailing from China via the Cape of Good Hope. It was with a sense of personal tragedy that the islanders heard the news on 30th December 1672 that, in a great storm, lightning had struck the keep and magazine of Castle Cornet during the night. The explosion destroyed the keep and some of the Governor's private apartments. Among others the Governor's wife and mother were killed, but Hatton himself escaped alive, though he was blown in his bed onto the battlements.

This disaster was followed by public mourning in the island and by the increased interest of the English Government in the island's defences. Castle Cornet was now useless as the Governor's residence, but the repairs to it as a fortress were undertaken by the Ordnance Department, a considerable financial relief to the islanders. Repairs too were carried out to Jerbourg Castle, which was equipped with gun platforms, and an engineers' survey of the island was ordered by Lord Dartmouth. The engineers recommended that Grande Havre Bay should be converted to a great harbour for an English fleet. However nothing came of this as Charles's Exchequer was virtually empty, and his only paymaster was England's enemy, Louis XIV.

At this time the placid existence of Sark was disturbed by a constitutional question. At the Restoration the seigneur, de Carteret, had returned to his fief, and the farming and fishing community went on its uneventful way. A visitor to the island in 1673 described it in a letter as a placid place, where the sandy soil produced parsnips, carrots and turnips, where apple trees grew with rich crops, where sheep for wool and milking cows grazed. The islanders lived mainly on what they caught, shot or snared, fish, woodcock, wild duck, pigeon, and rabbits, especially from Brechou Island. Dressed in their distinctive costume, the men in vast blue trunk breeches, and a coat like a Dutch frau's vest, the women in hospital gowns of blue, wooden sandals, white stockings, and red petticoats, they gathered in groups in the barns to knit the woollen stockings. A piper and old songs accompanied their work. Dean de Sausmarez's Anglicanism did not appear to have reached them, for a Huguenot minister had lately begun to teach the children grammar.

At the time of this peaceful scene a hundred-years-old quarrel between the Sarkese and the Guernsey authorities was resolved. Helier de Carteret had set up his own Bench of Jurats, but difficulties arose. The Guernseymen were jealous of this independence, it was difficult to find men of the calibre for the post, and such jurats as there were refused to take the oath to the Guernsey Governor. In 1675 the office of Sark jurat was abolished and the island was given a new constitution, with the Seigneur at the head, the Sénéschal, or Judge, and the officers of the Court of Chief Pleas, to be the island's governing and judicial body.

At this time Sir Edmund Andros succeeded his father as Bailiff of Guernsey. He was one of the first islanders to make a career in what might be called the embryonic colonial service. Brought up with the royal family, he had close links with the Stuarts, and had served under Prince Henry of Nassau. He rose to a position of great power in the North American colonies, first as Governor of New York and New England, and later as Governor of Virginia and Maryland, duties which he carried out in an efficient but wholly autocratic manner. 'Andros was as arbitrary as the Grand Turk,' wrote one contemporary. So that it was as well for Guernsey that he did not return to the island until Queen Anne's reign, when he was appointed Lieutenant-Governor as well as Bailiff. However, from across the Atlantic he kept in touch with events, and his powerful influence was available to help the islanders at need, for departments of the English

Government were always ready to interfere. As early as 1681 the Customs Commissioners, aware of the growth of a profitable smuggling trade between the Islands and ports in the West Country, tried to control it. A Customs officer was sent to Jersey to check up on the loading and unloading of tobacco. His fate was to be set upon and beaten, and to receive no help or sympathy from the island authorities. For the moment this interference was abandoned.

In a second sphere of island activity, the knitting trade, the helpful influence of important men was welcome. The merchants and knitters were passing through a difficult period, for their markets had been gravely interrupted by the Civil Wars, and when after 1660 they tried to expand again, they met with French competition, restrictions imposed by Louis XIV's Government, and a cut in the quota of wool licensed to be imported from England. Hints of their struggles can be gleaned from the papers of the de Sausmarez family, who with the Dobrées were the leading Guernsey merchants. Matthew de Sausmarez attended to the Guernsey end of the business, using his very competent wife, Bertranne, to deal with the individual knitters in their cottages. As agent in Paris, he had his brother Michael, and other agents in St. Malo, Coutances, Rouen, and Bordeaux. Many were the crises, of competition, change of fashion, trade restriction, or threat of war. But the brothers struggled on to sell their three main lines: Bas à Hommes, Rhingraves, or petticoat breeches, and Bas à Canon, long thigh-length stockings, of many colours, with attractive names—Rejoicing Widow, Dying Monkey, Amorous Desire, Sad Friend, Mortal Sin. The prices ranged from £3 10s. to £6 10s. per pair.

Perhaps the influence of the Andros family, and of Prince Rupert, then Lord High Admiral of England, for whom de Sausmarez procured a fur-lined bonnet, prevailed in high places. At any rate a petition of 1686 was granted, and the quota of wool to be exported to the Islands was increased, 4,000 tods for Jersey, 2,000 for Guernsey, double the quota allowed in Charles II's reign. From this time the 'lazy industry', as Jurat Poingdestre of Jersey called it, for it drew whole families away from agriculture, prospered for about one hundred years, until changing tastes and the call of more exciting business led to its decline, but not its death. Today the 'Jersey' is still a household word, and the 'Guernsey', knitted in one piece on twelve needles, is a highly prized garment.

Besides the threat to the labour force, there was a second cause of change in the traditional agricultural system. Cider became the staple drink of the islanders, one contemporary Jersey historian reckoning that 24,000 hogsheads were made every year. To supply the apples, great apple orchards were planted, in little fields enclosed by high banks of earth, on which the frugal farmers planted furze for fuel.

The more aggressive spirit shown by the French, stirred by the European reputation of Louis XIV and the successes of his diplomacy and armies, affected the Jerseymen in Newfoundland. There they fought a lonely battle, largely unsupported by the Government at home, against continuous French encroachments on their fishing grounds and store sites. It was a very serious situation for an island so heavily committed to this trade, as so many of their men made a livelihood from it to complement the living that their families got from the land. No figures are available for this period, but one hundred years later the Jersey Lieutenant-Governor wrote 'as near 1,300 men yearly go to Newfoundland for the fishery'.

It was then in an uneasy period of change, threat and struggle that news began to leak through of James II's Popish plans. The islanders had already been intensely moved by the stories of persecution in France after the Revocation of the Edict of Nantes in 1685. They had also seen the practical results, when some thousands of Huguenot refugees arrived, to be given a friendly welcome. Many settled in the Islands, to found notable island families. The story of Daniel Guerin may serve to illustrate their adventures. He came from a steadfast Protestant family of Guienne, and escaped arrest by Louis's soldiers to get away through many dangers across the Pyrenees to Spain and then on to Lisbon. As he stood on the quay he saw a ship flying the British flag. Yet the sailors spoke in French. He discovered they were from Guernsey and were loading wine for Messrs. Carey, an island wine business. One of the partners, Pierre Martin, saw him as he stood there, talked to him, and invited him back to Guernsey. There he joined the firm, made his way, and established a well-known local family.

The islanders had their own strong Protestant traditions, and together with their fear of an aggressive Catholic France, and these examples in their midst of the victims of that faith triumphant, the actions of James made the situation appear grim indeed. He appointed Catholic Governors for Jersey and Guernsey, and sent over Catholic captains and Irish troops with their chaplains to form a large part of the garrisons. When William of Orange landed in Torbay in November 1688, the situation became tenser still, especially in Jersey, for they could remember how Charles II had tried to hold out there. Might his brother, backed by French troops, try to seize the castles as a Stuart rallying-point?

A Jacobite plot in Jersey was foiled, as the two ringleaders, a priest and a St. Malo merchant, were both seized, on the orders of the States, in spite of complete non-co-operation from the Catholic captain. Then the Lieutenant-Governor, Philippe le Geyt, made things safer by persuading the captain to allow a proportion of the militia to enter the castles and mount guard with the regulars.

At last in April 1689 Sir Bevil Granville, nephew of Sir Edouard de Carteret, arrived from England, in command of a loyal regiment. 'The Papists were disarmed', says Falle, a local historian, 'and the island secured for the Prince.'

In Guernsey the details were different, but the result was the same. There the island leaders made a plan with the senior Protestant officer. When it was this officer's day to command the garrison, the captain of the town militia seized and disarmed the Catholic officers and soldiers who were found in the town. In the castle the garrison commander paraded his men. Suddenly the Protestants, their muskets loaded with ball, moved forward and swung to face the other troops, intimidating them into laying down their arms.

The revolution which replaced James II's kingship by the joint rule of William III and Mary was thus carried through in the Islands, as it was in England. The most immediate effect of the accession of William, dedicated as he was to a lifelong struggle against the imperialism of Louis XIV, was his decision to end the Islands' two-hundred-year-old Treaty of Neutrality. By prohibiting 'the importation of any commodities of the growth or manufacture of France' he stopped legal trade during the war.

This action was not as serious in its consequences for the island merchants as might appear. For they had a well-tried outlet—smuggling. The Ecrehos rocks, off Jersey, became the market-place of Jersey and French seamen and traders, and all attempts to stop the traffic failed, for everyone from the Lieutenant-Governor downwards was involved in the profitable business. Almost as profitable was the smuggling trade from Guernsey and Jersey to England, and over this the Customs Commissioners had no more success.

The other outlet was privateering. Although in the past the Islands had strictly speaking been covered by the Bull of Neutrality, there had been privateers before the time of William of Orange. The earliest recorded privateer was John Briard, a Guernsey merchant and owner of the *Dove*, who received a Letter of Marque from Queen Elizabeth to attack French shipping in 1598. There had been George Carteret's privateer fleet of the Civil Wars, and in the French War of 1667 John Tupper of Guernsey operated as a privateer.

Now, however, it was both profitable and recognized as

legal. Yet the islanders embarked on this adventure, so dangerous, but in the end so profitable, with considerable caution. Their captains and seamen were not experienced in this type of action, the French fleet held the Channel for two years after the battle of Beachy Head, and the English Government did not encourage them. They were obstructed in their efforts to dispose of their prize cargoes profitably in English markets, and the Government demanded the payment of a tenth of the prize money to the Admiralty.

Greater opportunity came to them after 1692. In that year Louis XIV made preparations to send across a great army from Normandy, which was to be covered by a French fleet of forty-five sail coming up from Brest. The English were aware of these preparations, and English and Dutch fleets converged on the area, to fight a successful running action, and drive the French fleet into the harbours of Cherbourg and La Hogue, where James II had to stand on the cliffs and watch the destruction. In the mopping-up operations John Tupper, commander of the Guernsey privateer, *Monmouth Galley*, destroyed four French privateers as they tried to escape through the Alderney Race. His reward was a gold medal and chain, and a public citation for his action.

This naval victory ended the striking power of the French Navy for many years, and left the seas to be controlled by the British and Dutch fleets. It also left French seaborne trade at the mercy of the privateer. The islanders took advantage of this, and by the end of the war in 1697 some thirty Guernsey and eight Jersey privateers were in operation. These were small beginnings, but it was a valuable apprenticeship for the sea captains.

The La Hogue victory marked too the end of an era in the Islands' history. The previous period had been an uneasy one, with threats of invasion, a Catholic menace, uncertainty and revolution in England, bitter Protestant quarrels, threats of interference by England with their time-honoured rights and institutions, and struggling trade. In the future down to the oubreak of the American war in 1776 there were to be further dangers, feuds and difficulties, but it was to be a comparatively tranquil and prosperous period.

There was little danger from threats from France, as the Islands were protected overall by the watching power of the British Navy. They had also their own militias, citizen forces well-equipped and drilled, under their own officers. In 1750 the Guernsey Militia was a force of fifty-four officers and nearly two thousand N.C.O.s and men, divided into three regiments. The leading families were proud to serve, and at this date two of the colonels were Le Marchants, and one an Andros. There was some local suspicion that the Lieutenant-Governor, Spicer, was selling too many commissions, and some jealousy between the officers of the old-established infantry companies and those of the newly formed artillery companies. With the outbreak of the Seven Years War most of this ill-feeling faded, when officers and men were ready for their duty, to mount night-watches at the watch-houses round the coast, to man the guns on the batteries, to keep themselves ready by intensive drill, and to be prepared to turn out at a moment's notice. The Island's pride in them was shown in 1761, when a large area above the town, known as the New Ground, was bought as a drill ground for the Town Regiment and as a pleasant place for the citizens to stroll.

There was little interference from England in their affairs. The Governors were absentees, the Lieutenant-Governors often nonentities, and the great Tory and Whig gentlemen were not concerned with such remote and possibly barbarous places. The Islands were again successful in 1709 in resisting an attempt by the Customs Commissioners to impose their rules on the islands' trade, and Guernsey a few years later countered the objections of jealous Southampton merchants and secured confirmation of her ancient right to bring her produce and manufactures freely into England.

Besides the economic one, the other reason for possible interference by the English Government was to settle internal feuds which might threaten the internal order and security of the Islands.

There seems to have been little occasion for this in Guernsey's story. The island government was virtually an oligarchy of the leading families, who had common interests and were often connected by inter-marriage. Provided they ran the island's affairs in a reasonably efficient and public-spirited way, there was little cause for popular unrest, and little scope either, as the jurats were elected by the States, in which the constables, the parish representatives, carried little weight. Only two occasions of trouble are recorded, one at the beginning of this period and one at the very end, in the 1770's, when a party of jurats protested against the all-embracing power of the bailiff. Queen Anne dismissed the petition against Bailiff Eleazar Le Marchant, but George III accepted that Bailiff William Le Marchant had exceeded his powers in deciding legal cases and other island matters without consulting the jurats. This quarrel continued for twenty years; on one occasion the Procureur, Thomas de Sausmarez, fought a duel with Robert Le Marchant, son of the bailiff.

For one reason or another, the feuds in Jersey were more bitter and more widespread. Possibly the landed families with their bigger estates felt themselves to be more of a nobility. Possibly the insignificance of St. Helier and St. Aubin meant that they had no common meeting-ground, where they would be forced to rub shoulders with the citizens on more or less equal terms. One definite opening for political strife lay in the fact that the Jersey jurats were elected by popular vote in the parishes.

The general unrest first showed itself in strong objections from the tenants to the payment of their seigneurial dues. This particularly involved the bailiff, Sir Charles de Carteret, who, when the King's Council decided against his opinions, faltered to his death, in 1715, the last of the direct line of de Carterets who had passed the fief on from father to son for seven hundred years.

The petty bickering and decline in morale was increased by hostility between the clergy and the laity; this centred on the battle for authority between the jurats and Royal Court and the Dean and Ecclesiastical Court. Many were the rectors who found themselves in the town gaol, and many were the officials, jurats, constables and others who were excommunicated.

Matters came to a head in 1730. For some years difficulties had arisen over the monetary situation. The value of French coins was falling steadily, and yet the Jerseymen, whose main trade in the periods of peace was with Normandy, used a similar coinage, the liard, the sol, and the livre tournois. The shrewd Normans insisted on being paid in silver, but paid their bills in bags of depreciating liards. Thus the island was being drained of good coinage. To counter this the States secured an Order in Council from England devaluing the liard by one-third. This order caused 'the greatest riot ever known in Jersey', as the thrifty farmer and the struggling debtor suddenly found his fortune cut or his debt increased. A mob of three hundred stormed the house of the Lieutenant-Bailiff, Philippe le Geyt, and threatened to hang him. The next day a bigger demonstration was staged, when the parishes rallied behind their militia drummers to march on the town and rush the court-house, crying, 'Death to the Six au Sols,' although the States had hurriedly passed an Act restoring the liard to its former value.

George II was angry at this defiance of his Order and sent over four hundred troops. But an opposition Popular Party began to form, led by a young advocate, Jean Dumaresq. Amid scenes of great confusion he was elected a jurat, and when he and his supporters had a majority in the Royal Court, and then in the States, they set to work to deal with some of the island's wrongs, the devaluing of the liard and the practice of farming out to speculators the collection of tithes. The King was prevailed on to dismiss Dumaresq and his supporting jurats, and gradually the excitement died down.

But the islanders did not forget the insult of 'Six au Sol', the implication that a few rich men were out to exploit the poor, and a critical revolutionary spirit was born. This spirit found fresh grist to its mill during the bailiffship of Charles Lemprière. He was appointed Lieutenant-Bailiff in 1750, but, as in that easy-going era the Earls Granville passed the post of bailiff on from heir to heir and never visited the island, he was the virtual ruler. Supported by a majority of relatives in the Royal Court, he built up a dictatorship, issuing ordinances through the Court, and through it punishing those who resisted.

Opposition centred at first on Fiott, a tough sea captain, who quarrelled with Lemprière and found himself in gaol. Only a monster petition from the poorer Jerseymen helped to secure his release.

More widespread trouble started in 1769 over the price of corn. As it was common practice for loans to farmers to be made against a wheat rente, or mortgage, it followed that when the price of corn rose, the rich man's income rose too. At this date the States, who had prohibited the export of corn during a number of lean years, allowed it again. The price soared and popular discontent boiled over. The men of the parishes marched on the town and forced the jurats to pass an ordinance reducing the price of wheat and the charge of Crown tithes, abolishing the seigneurs, right to champart, the wheat tax, and securing the banishment of all aliens and the cancellation of all charges against Fiott. This outbreak bore all the marks of an organized movement. Lemprière and his jurats escaped via Elizabeth Castle to England, and on hearing their tale of revolution the King's Council sent over Colonel Bentinck and five companies of the Royal Scots to keep order.

Bentinck discovered that there was another side to the story, and went round the parishes hearing complaints at the Parish Assemblies. Meanwhile two half-pay officers, Corbet and Le Geyt, organized another monster petition and crossed to England to present it to the King. Further pressure was brought to bear on Lemprière by Le Geyt's father-in-law, John Shebbeare, a violent English pamphleteer, who issued two pamphlets, 'An Authentic Narrative of the Oppression of the Islanders of Jersey' and 'The Tyranny of the Magistrates of Jersey'. Another blow fell when Bentinck was made Lieutenant-Governor, with orders to pacify the island and introduce the necessary reforms. The result was an Order in Council, approved by the Jersey States, which deprived the Royal Court of its ancient right to legislate, and which confirmed that power to the States. It also forbade the practice of farming out the Crown revenue, and it ordered the codification of the island laws for the first time in its history.

Even in Sark there was a minor crisis about half-way through the century. The Anglican Church tended to solve the problem of the supply of French-speaking parsons by appointing to livings lapsed French Catholics, some of whom were persons of doubtful value. The Dame of Sark, Susan le Pelley, into whose hands the seigneurial rights had passed, disapproved of the rector, one of these men, and, exercising her authority, she locked the church door and refused to allow the building to be used for any purpose whatever. Letters, orders and threats of excommunication from the Dean of Guernsey failed to move her. At last the problem was solved by the Bishop of Winchester, who produced a new minister acceptable to all parties.

In spite of these periodic disturbances, the economies of the Islands improved steadily. The Jersey-Newfoundland fishing industry was helped and protected by the Treaty of Utrecht, which ended the French claim to Newfoundland, though for a time they continued to share in the fishing. But the islanders now had the British Government and the Navy behind them and during the wars of this century French competition was slowly strangled. The one serious threat arose from the policy of George III's Government, which in 1768 passed an Act requiring all Channel Island vessels to be cleared from a British port. This infringed the Islands' charters and the Jersey Chamber of Commerce was formed to fight the regulation. After a long struggle it was withdrawn, and direct trade was allowed again.

The fishing industry was Jersey's main overseas venture, but at home her agriculture prospered. The acreage under wheat, for home consumption and export, declined slightly, but this was compensated for by the big increase in cider-production, much of which was exported. A technical advance was made in the sixties in the husbandry of the main crop, parsnips. A Jersey farmer invented the 'Grande Charrue', the great plough for deep tilling of the soil, which replaced the back-breaking labour with spades. This plough was a communal tool, which might be pulled by as many as twenty-two beasts, sixteen oxen and six horses, the farmers of an area pooling their resources. When the ploughing was over for the day and the work completed, everyone involved adjourned to the farmhouse for a feast of celebration, which was followed by singing and games. Plenty of cider was drunk. 'One must take a sip to moisten the field or there will be no parsnips.'

Another increase in the farmers' income came from improvements in the Islands' breeds of cattle. Milk production rose, and a start was made in the export of selected beasts to Southampton. A favourite of the English novelists of the time was the Alderney cow.

This prosperity gave a chance to the more enterprising farming families to improve their living conditions. Many a solid granite farmhouse was built during these years for the *chefs de famille*, the principal rate-payers, from among whom the douzeniers or centeniers, the churchwardens, and the country jurats were chosen. The houses were built to a pattern, low, with three-foot thick walls of red and blue granite, roofed with thatch or red pantiles, with nine windows, five upstairs and four down. The living-room-kitchen was the family room, where the cooking was done in the large open fireplace or in the bread-oven. In this room the family gathered at the oblong deal table. Against the walls stood the green bed and the dresser, and hanging from the ceiling were the bacon rack and the bread rack. Across the hall was the parlour, reserved for ceremonial occasions, such as funerals. An important addition to the farm buildings at this time was *le pressoir,* where the great oak cider-press and the circular granite cider trough were kept.

More important mansions were built on their estates by some of the leading families. In Guernsey the Le Marchants built Saumarez Park at this time, and enlarged and altered the old Henry house at La Haye du Puits. The Guilles improved St. George, and in the same area was another fine estate, Woodlands, where in the large orchards grew the Mollet Pippin, La Pomme Susanne, an outstanding cider apple first developed by a Jersey fruit-grower and cider-maker.

Some of these families had their town houses, too, mostly in the High Street, and there the well-to-do gathered to entertain each other in a simple kindly way. There was little of the extravagance of the English aristocracy, as can be gathered from the accounts for an entertainment for Prince William and two hundred guests when he visited the island. Tea and coffee, £4 18s. Candles, £2 16s. Lemons and sugar for Punch and Negus, 19s. 3d. Twelve packs of cards, 9s. Two pairs of gloves for H.R.H., 3s. One set of fish lost for quadrille, 9s. 6d. Wine, £7 11s. 6d. Confectionery, £9 3s. 8d. Music, £4 13s. Breakage, 18s. 6d. Corkage on wine, £1 0s. 3d. Rooms and attendance, £3 3s. Total, £36 4s. 8d.

The sons of such families, especially in Guernsey, tended to be sent to school in England for a year or two, to supplement the rather rudimentary education, to widen their outlook, and to improve their English, before they either returned to their island, to take up their careers, or went into the Royal Navy or the Army. Some, on their return, tended to despise the simpler island life. One young man appeared to have forgotten his patois completely and his father was in despair. How could he help run the farm when he could not talk to the labourers? One day the young fellow, passing through the farmyard, put his foot on a rake hidden in the straw. 'An Guyablle siet le râté', (Devil take the rake), he forgot himself and shouted. His father was delighted and begged him not to 'forget his rake'. This saying became an island proverb.

One of the most notable of the sons who in this period went into the Services was Philip de Sausmarez. He and his brother Thomas, following the example of their Jersey cousins, the Durells, joined the Navy. They were both picked for service in the squadron under George Anson, which the Admiralty sent off in 1740 to sail round the Horn and to 'vex' the Spaniards. After many adventures, much suffering and great heroism, they arrived back with Anson in the *Centurion* three years and nine months later, after circumnavigating the globe, capturing the *Manila Galleon* and taking treasure worth £600,000. Their triumphant reception in London recalled the days of Drake and the great sea-dogs. Sadly Philip's career ended in a naval battle off Brest, when he was shot. But he had made his mark, not only as one of the most brilliant of the new type of naval officer, but also as the designer of the uniform which George II chose as most suitable for naval officers.

The islanders were proud of his achievements, but his share of the prize-money had a further result. It enabled his family to buy back the ancient manor from the Andros family, who had held it for two hundred years or more and who only agreed to sell as the present owner was childless. Strangely, only a year after the sale, Madame Andros bore a son; she was so bitter over the premature sale that she cursed the mill of Sausmarez—'Never again shall it grind the tenants' oats or the seigneur's wheat.' The old mill was left to become a derelict landmark.

In a sense Anson's voyage was privateering on the grand scale. It was from more modest efforts, legal or illegal, that the island merchants and seamen accumulated considerable sums during this time. To them legitimate trading, privateering and smuggling were only different aspects of the attempt to win wealth from foreigners.

In all these branches of trade the men of Guernsey played a leading part. They were much less involved in the Newfoundland fisheries than the Jerseymen, they had the advantages of geographical position and of a good harbour and roadstead, and they worked together, merchants, seamen, landed men with capital, to exploit the situation to the utmost.

The legitimate trade was at first confined to French ports, such as St. Malo, and to Southampton. Small coasters made the trips, averaging three sailings a week, and carrying such cargoes as cider, stones, lobsters, knitted goods, cattle and wine. Later the merchants and the sea captains, who were often also their agents, expanded their activities, and a regular circular traffic grew up. A typical cruise of one of these merchant adventurers followed this course. He sailed with brandy to Madeira, where it was bartered for wine. Then away across to the West Indies, to barter the wine for rum to carry to Newfoundland. The rum was then bartered for fish, which was carried back to the Mediterranean and Portuguese ports. Of the firms which engaged in such traffic the greatest was Carteret Priaulx, which had been founded in 1712, and by the seventies owned twelve privateers and had business connections all over Europe and America.

With the small accumulations of capital which such merchants had made in the reign of William and Mary from the sale of captured French wines and brandies, they exploited the favourable situation created by the fact that St. Peter Port was a free port, where English and French merchants could deposit their goods without the payment of duty until the favourable moment for a sale arrived. An accident of climate helped in this, for it was found that the temperature in the vaults of the Town was ideal for the storage and maturing of wines and spirits. One islander who no doubt was very well aware of this was Jean Martel, a Jerseyman, who after an apprenticeship to the wine trade in Guernsey

7 Market-place, Guernsey, *circa* 1830

8 The Liberation Fleet off St. Peter Port, 9th May 1945 (*by permission of* C. *Toms Esq.*)

emigrated to France, and settled down with a French Protestant wife in the Cognac area, an area where he recognized the superlative quality of the brandies. His firm prospered and developed wide connections, with the Hansa Towns, with Holland, and with the Islands. Significantly he had no direct trade links with England.

The vaults to store these wines, spirits and other goods were dug out from the cliffs, or built, all over St. Peter Port; in fact, when all this trade was at its height the goods were sometimes stored in the fields for want of anywhere else to put them. Clearly such storage was not used for legitimate trade alone. Although for obvious reasons the records for the smuggling trade are scanty, it is known that much larger quantities of wine and spirits were brought into Guernsey than the official records show to have been taken out again. A local historian comments: 'The chief entrepot for the smuggling trade with England during the greater part of the eighteenth century and the early years of the nineteenth was the Channel Isles, and of this very lucrative business Guernsey monopolized by far the larger share.' Not that the islanders themselves took much part in the actual smuggling. They held the goods, which the English 'free-traders' came to carry away, and they defended this practice against the English Customs officials with two strong arguments. They argued first that their privileges gave them a right to a free port, and second that it was better that the profits from smuggling, which was inevitable as the English Government increased the duties on imported articles, should be shared among the Crown's subjects rather than diverted to aliens and enemies.

In the third branch of their business on the seas, privateering, the islanders played their part adventurously, often heroically, and in general honourably. Putting the experience gained in William III's war to good effect, the privateers from Guernsey and Jersey made a considerable contribution to the Grand Alliance, and to the misery of France in the declining years of Louis XIV. With their remarkable knowledge of the French coast, the reefs of Brittany, the Bay of Biscay, and the Gironde, they disrupted the French coastal trade, on which in the absence of good roads the French economy in the area depended. Not only did they sweep the seas, but they crept in to ambush convoys, to cut out ships at anchor, and to raid rivers, harbours and roadsteads. As they grew more successful, their numbers increased and by the end of the War of the Spanish Succession there were 115 Guernsey and 51 Jersey privateers in operation. The biggest of these were the *Marquis D'Or* and the *Guernsey Frigate,* both of 200 tons, with an armament of between 12 and 20 guns, but for attack they largely relied on boarding, with small arms and cutlasses. The financial success of their operations may be judged from the record, that up to 1711 Jersey privateers had taken 151 and Guernsey privateers 608 prizes, and the value of the Guernsey prizes has been estimated at up to £100,000.

While England was at peace these privateers were laid up, or sold for smuggling, or used for legitimate trading. When England went to war with France again in the Seven Years War, out they came in force. This time they were joined by privateers from Alderney.

Over Alderney the Governor, Sir Edmund Andros, had appointed a Guernseyman, Thomas le Mesurier, as his Lieutenant-Governor in 1713, and it was this family which inherited the Governorship eight years later. A long and bitter feud broke out between the Governor and the local family of Le Cocq, led by the island judge, and this lasted until the judge was suspended from office. The intransigence of the Alderney people continued, however, and Thomas's son, Henry, was only too happy to exchange his troubled position for some land in Guernsey with his brother John. John le Mesurier was made of sterner stuff, and although he had to flee once for his life, he returned and gradually won over the islanders. Andros had tried to solve Alderney's overpopulation by sending poor children out to New Jersey, but John built the first breakwater at the Braye harbour, and fitted out privateers manned by Alderney seamen. Not only was there privateering in wartime, but there were profits to be made from smuggling, and the local population developed a specialized trade, the making of the small kegs, so handy for a rocky cliff path in the dark. To show his confidence in the island, John built himself Mouriaux House, in the little town of St. Anne and later, improvements were made to the church and to the court-house. A lucrative and hopeful period had begun in the island's chequered history.

Chapter 9

The French Wars

In March 1778 George III's Government, already shaken by the surrender of General Burgoyne to the Americans at Saratoga, found themselves faced by war with France and Spain as well. The Bourbon Powers had waited a long time for such an opportunity of revenge, and they took it at a moment when they were not hampered by any continental entanglements themselves.

This situation, while it gave the islanders the openings for privateering which they had accepted eagerly in previous wars, yet was a grave threat to them too. For owing to Sandwich's incompetence the British Navy was weak compared to the combined French and Spanish fleets, and its central direction was muddled and inadequate. The islanders then could not rely as before on its protection, while the French, in aggressive mood, knew well the terrible damage that the island privateers had inflicted before. The Governor of Cherbourg reported, 'These two islands are the despair of France, at the breaking out of each war, through their remarkably active privateers. The habit of encountering the dangers of the sea renders the natives very brave. They have well-disciplined regiments of militia, excellent marksmen. They are always in a state of warfare, now against the custom-house officers of the two kingdoms, now against the French commercial marine. A population of this character greatly enhances the natural strength of these islands.'

The Governor was right, and another report of his for the year 1778 showed how quickly the islanders had gone into action. 'There are in St. Helier's roads more than 15 French prizes, and in the island 1,500 seamen, prisoners.' The rewards were enormous. It has been calculated that in 1778 £343,500 was brought in as prizes by twenty privateers, in 1779 £270,000 by six, and in 1782 £156,500 by five. One of the most successful was John le Mesurier of Alderney, whose ship the *Resolution*, of twenty guns with a crew of a hundred, brought in £134,500 in 1779. By 1782 he had built up his fleet to eight ships, and his total prize-money for that year had reached £212,000. Another Guernseyman, John Tupper, with three ships collected prizes worth nearly £60,000. A third successful privateer was the lugger, *Alarm*, carrying fourteen guns and with a crew of fifty-six; her principal owner was John Henry, the King's Receiver, and she turned out a good investment, with seven prizes of a gross value of £38,500. In all it is reckoned that the total value of prizes in the war came to over £900,000.

Not content with sweeping the seas the privateers also made land raids. It was reported that Jersey privateers landed near Caen, and carried off oxen, cows, sheep, and all the curé's washing, including the two washerwomen.

It was not surprising that the French prepared for revenge, choosing to attack Jersey, partly because it lay nearer, partly perhaps because the internal struggle there between the bailiff, Lemprière, and his popular opponent, Jean Dumaresq, made the situation appear more hopeful. Jean Dumaresq's party was nicknamed the Magots, as one of Charles Lemprière's supporters, a Charlot, had threatened to squash them like cheese-mites. 'We may be maggots,' replied Dumaresq, 'but we will make these seigneurs bite the dust.' Every election was fought with great ferocity, and by 1781 Dumaresq had a majority on the Jersey States, and it was clear that he would soon have one in the Royal Court too. Charles Lemprière read the signs, and, passing on his post to his son, William, he retired to England.

The first French attempt in May 1779 was a complete failure, as the garrison and the militia were ready to receive them, and the Frenchmen argued, the warships refusing to come in close enough to cover the landing, the troopships refusing to come in range of the shore batteries. The expedition withdrew discomfited to St. Malo, where five of the warships were destroyed at anchor by a British squadron.

However the threat galvanized the British Government into action to strengthen the defences. The garrisons were increased, and work was put in hand to construct Fort George in Guernsey, on the heights commanding the harbour and roadstead, with an outlier at Clarence Battery. It was to be a small quadrangular fortress with four bastions, and the construction was pushed ahead so feverishly that it was completed in three years.

Other defensive measures included the building of Martello Towers to guard possible landing places and of other small forts on the headlands. There was even a fort north of St. Peter Port which was erected by public subscription and which was presented to the States. Aptly enough it was named Fort Subscription. Another ingenious idea of the Guernsey Royal Court caused great ill feeling. They passed an ordinance that the militia should wear red coats so as to look to the enemy like soldiers of the line. The parishes objected strongly, that they were a citizen militia, serving without pay, and most of them could not afford such finery. The problem was solved eventually by the English Government, which sent over the uniforms.

The French did not abandon their plan to counter-attack. A second expedition was prepared under the formidable leadership of a soldier of fortune, the Baron de Rullecourt. He crossed secretly to Jersey, disguised as a grain-smuggler, and spied out the best landing-places. The Jerseymen had no inkling of these preparations, and on the night of 5th January 1781 Rullecourt brought his twenty-six boats safely through a narrow channel and landed them at La Rocque. The militia guard had gone home and Rullecourt was able to bring ashore 600 men quite undetected. The remainder had to put to sea again, owing to a change of tide, but he and his 600 marched secretly into the town before sunrise. With this small force he almost succeeded in bluffing the surrender of the island, then garrisoned by 1,000 Regulars and 3,000 militiamen. He caught the Lieutenant-Governor, Corbet, in his house, and by saying that he held the island and would burn down the town, he induced him to send orders that all should lay down their arms.

But the Jersey forces were already taking action. The castle guns opened fire on the French. The Highlanders, who were reinforced by some militiamen, took up position on Gallows Hill, and from St. Peters Francis Pierson, a young major of twenty-four, led his half of the 24th Foot to join them. As the force on Gallows Hill thus grew to 1,600 men the orders arrived from Corbet to surrender. Pierson was not sure whether Corbet was acting under duress. Then Corbet himself arrived under parole to insist on obedience. This was more than Pierson was prepared to submit to; he told the Lieutenant-Governor bluntly that he would die rather than surrender. Using covering fire from the site of Fort Regent, he organized skilful converging attacks on the market-place, where the French were massed. The battle was quickly over, but both the leaders, Pierson and Rullecourt, were killed. Although Corbet by taking charge did his best to redeem his reputation, a court-martial followed. His plea that his order was a ruse to save the town and give his troops time to regroup was generally accepted, but he was dismissed from his post in Jersey. Elisha Dobrée, the Guernsey diarist, recorded 'Good news of the defeat of French in Jersey'.

The signing of the Treaty of Versailles brought relief to the islanders, for the hard-worked militia could now relax, the threat of attack was past, and the merchants and fishermen could sail the seas without fear of being snapped up by a French privateer. But the island privateer owners, captains and crews waited expectantly for other opportunities.

While England and France and Spain were locked in the battle for empire, new ideas and emotions were moving the minds and hearts of men, the ideas of the French Philosophes, of Benjamin Franklin, of Tom Paine. Sympathy with these ideas was partly responsible for the success of Jean Dumaresq's Magots in Jersey. There William Lemprière, the new Lieutenant-Bailiff, was even more of an autocrat than his father, treating the Jersey States as a consultative committee, while to Dumaresq the States was the Assembly in which the whole legislative power of the island resided. The struggle raged on. Dumaresq was helped by two factors, the election of the jurats by popular vote, and the support of the new three-sous weekly newspaper, *Gazette de L'Ile de Jersey*. At last, in 1790, the Magots had a majority in the Court as well as in the States; the People's Party had won, and fittingly in the same year William Lemprière died.

Besides this stirring of democracy in Jersey, the Islands were influenced by the great Protestant religious revival of the time, the Methodist movement. In 1783 an English regiment was posted for service in Jersey and some of the troops were Methodists. They found that all the services were in French, and they wrote appealing to John Wesley, 'the greatest Protestant force of the eighteenth century', as Birrell summed him up. Wesley sent over an ardent young lay preacher, Brackenbury, the Squire of Raithby, who was fortunately bilingual. He started services at 3 Royal Square, St. Helier, and gradually the movement spread.

After a year in France to improve his French, Brackenbury returned to Jersey, where he was greatly helped by a young islander, Jean de Quetteville. By 1785 the first stirrings of the movement had spread to Guernsey, and Brackenbury was invited to visit there and preach. After this initial success he consulted Dr. Coke, one of Wesley's leading assistants who had already organized the Methodist Church in America. Coke crossed swiftly to Jersey and the two decided to follow this up by sending over young de Quetteville, the only bilingual preacher free to go to Guernsey, who found he had eighteen converts. Among them was a well-to-do gentleman, Henry de Jersey, whose house,

Mon Plaisir, became the headquarters of the Movement. De Quetteville was soon joined in his mission by Adam Clarke, an able preacher, whose French was not good enough for Jersey, whereas in Guernsey there were many more who understood English. In spite of a threat from the Governor, Le Mesurier, that he would transport him to the Casquets, Clarke landed in Alderney, and there too he drew together the elements of a Methodist Society. In 1787 John Wesley himself went into action. He was now eighty-four, but quite undaunted he set sail from Southampton to visit this new and promising field. After a stormy passage he reached St. Peter Port in August and, staying at Mon Plaisir, he preached to large congregations. He was such a famous figure that the Lieutenant-Governor invited him to dine. His next port of call was Jersey, where he stayed seven days, preaching each day to further large congregations. His return to Southampton was diverted by storms back to Guernsey, where he had another week's preaching, to large numbers, both inside and outside, at Mon Plaisir, at the Assembly Rooms or out in the country. As he recorded in his *Journal*, 'They appeared to be more and more affected, so that I believe we were not detained for nothing.'

It was ironical that John Wesley should have been invited to meet an audience in the Assembly Rooms, for they were the cause of the main social disturbance in Guernsey at this time. A few years before, twenty of the ruling families had subscribed to build the Assembly Rooms, a fine Georgian building, with an arcade for a market beneath. The rules for admittance were very strict, and limited the entries to about sixty local families, and also the officers of the garrison and eligible English officials. This exclusiveness upset the families of the privateer-profiteers, who were furious at being blackballed, and a long-lasting feud developed between the 'Sixties' and the 'Forties', as the rejected were called, no doubt to the immense amusement of all the other islanders.

John Wesley's visit gave added impetus to the work in the Islands. Yet there was much persecution in the next few years. In Guernsey an attempt was made to banish de Quetteville; this failed as the bailiff, Le Marchant, was a fair-minded man. But in Jersey the authorities were violently hostile, the clergy preached against the Methodists, and the mob were encouraged to attack them. This persecution served to strengthen the members, and their influence spread with the building of the first chapel in Guernsey, in Rue Le Marchant, in 1789; it was a great thrill for the struggling society that the bailiff himself came to inspect the foundations. As the Jersey Royal Court refused to register the contract of sale of a plot of land to the Methodist Society there, their chapel was delayed until a year later, 1790. By this date the Movement was established and gradually gained a strong hold over the life of the Islands. Other chapels were built, another fourteen in Guernsey in the next seventy years. Methodism was a force to be reckoned with.

One particular problem which Methodism posed for the authorities in its early years arose over the Sunday drills of the militia. The Methodist militiamen objected strongly to this, and when they were fined and then imprisoned for absenteeism, their opposition only strengthened. In desperation the Jersey Government tried to suppress the Movement altogether, expelling all ministers and banishing all militiamen who refused to drill on Sundays. Appeals went to the King's Council, and to Wilberforce, to intercede for them, with complete success, for the oppressive orders were withdrawn and the Methodist militiamen were allowed to hold special drill parades on weekdays. In Alderney the Methodist contingent was mockingly nicknamed L'Armée du Gideon.

The efficiency of the local militias was a matter of considerable importance, for the great upheavals were taking place across the sea which were to lead to the French Revolution. At first the islanders looked on with some sympathy, for they had no love for the Bourbon Government. Yet they were not too pleased, especially in Jersey, when a flood of aristocratic refugees began to pour in. The local boatmen, it is true, made large sums from ferrying them across, and many of the *émigrés* brought over capital, in gold or jewels. With these reserves they built houses in the St. Helier area, trebling the size of the old town in a few years, but they were an uncertain and not altogether congenial new element in the population. The new Governor of Alderney, Peter Le Mesurier, had a special problem, as 124 French priests escaped there. He took them in and treated them with kindness, but he had to insist that they celebrated their rites in private, for the Alderney people were strongly Methodist.

The growing likelihood of war with revolutionary France caused Le Mesurier to reorganize the Alderney Militia. Up to his time the defence of the island had depended largely on the women, who, while the men worked, watched from the beacon towers, ready to light the fires to signal across to Guernsey. It was said that one French invading force earlier in the century had turned back when its commander saw the cliffs lined with red coats, these red coats being in fact the red skirts of the women.

At last Pitt was driven from his neutralist position by the aggressive actions and propaganda of the French Revolutionary Republic, and by the wave of horror which swept the country at the trial and execution of Louis XVI. He refused to recognize such a regime, and on 1st February 1793 the French Government declared war.

This put the Islands in the firing-line again. Out went the privateers, but the Committee of Public Safety was determined to crush this bastion of English power. They ordered the capture of the Channel Isles, and sent an army of 20,000 men to St. Malo to form the expeditionary force. Against this the island garrisons were strengthened, and the militias were alert and ready for the long period of watching and waiting which was to be their lot.

Yet it was the watchfulness of the Navy and the French Resistance Movement in Brittany and La Vendée which really prevented the full development of this dangerous French threat. One particular success which thrilled the

Guernseymen was the action carried out by Captain Sir James Saumarez in June 1794, to the north-west of the island. He had been sent out from Plymouth with three frigates to discover the size of the French naval forces in the St. Malo area. Running into a French squadron of superior numbers and firepower, he saved the other two frigates by drawing the French after his own ship, the *Crescent*. Piloted by a local man, Jean Breton, he got away through a narrow passage between the rocks. As the man-o'-war passed through, he asked the pilot if he were sure of his sea marks. 'I am quite sure, sir,' replied Breton, 'for there is your house and there is mine.'

But the man who did most to thwart the French was a Jerseyman, Philippe d'Auvergne, a naval officer, who commanded a small squadron of eight gunboats and kept a ceaseless watch on the invasion ports. He was a man of great ability, which probably explains the extraordinary situation that when a prisoner of war in French hands in the previous war he had been adopted by the old Prince Godfrey d'Auvergne, as heir to the Principality of Bouillon in the Belgian Ardennes. He was not content to organize his naval patrols. From his headquarters in Mont Orgueil he became the chief supplier of arms, ammunition and money to the Chouans, the resistance movement which sprang up in Brittany, and through them was in touch with the open revolt in La Vendée.

His Mont Orgueil headquarters served too as the centre for economic warfare against the French Republic; from there bales of forged notes were smuggled into France, to destroy confidence in the Republican paper money. An efficient spy system was based on there as well, by which d'Auvergne was able to report to the Admiralty details of the French fleets in Brest and other ports. This service he provided for the Admiralty was repaid, to Jersey's advantage, by the authority they gave him to organize naval convoys for the island's fishing and trading fleets to Newfoundland.

The *émigré* refugees were a problem to the authorities; they were restless, they were troublesome, and they tended to try to proselytize for their Roman Catholic faith. The English Government decided to make use of them in a landing in Brittany to help the Chouans. In Jersey 3,500 were enrolled, and a smaller contingent was collected in Guernsey. After many absurd problems had been solved, for instance that they all were determined to be colonels, the expedition was landed in Quiberon Bay in July 1795. One of the ablest Republican generals, Hoche, dealt with these amateur raiders, and the whole affair was a bloody and costly fiasco.

The French counter-attacked by sending agitators to Jersey to stir up the malcontents and by a second invasion plan in 1798; but nothing serious came of either threat. A greater danger came from Britain's allies, the Russians. After defeat in Holland, a Russian army had been evacuated, and as by the Bill of Rights it could not land in England, the only place to quarter it until the ice broke and the army could return through the Baltic to Russia, was the Channel Isles. Over 6,000 came to Jersey. The officers were charming, but the primitive soldiery took to highway robbery and burglary, and laid hands on all the raw spirits, lamp oil and tallow candles they could find.

About 6,000 camped in Guernsey too, on Delancey Heights. Of these some hundreds died of a fever, caught in the marshes of Holland. The survivors took to drinking raw spirits and plundering the nearby farms. Just before they re-embarked, one marauder was seen and shot. This roused the Russians and there was a tense scene. The guns of Castle Cornet were loaded, and only the tact of the Governor, Dalrymple, averted what might have become a very dangerous situation.

This shooting had a strange sequel. The farmer involved, Ogier, fled the island and eventually settled in Ohio. Prospering he encouraged his relatives from Guernsey to come out and join him, and this was the origin of Guernsey County.

Meanwhile the privateers continued their dangerous but profitable trade. By 1800 it was calculated that the money brought into Guernsey from French and American prizes totalled nearly a million pounds, and in that year thirty-five more ships were fitted out by the leading privateer speculators, which brought in another million. Some idea of the extent of the business can be obtained from the contemporary Journal of Elisha Dobrée, a Guernsey gentleman, a douzenier of the town parish and an Admiralty pilot, who was naturally interested in naval matters. His record for April 1793 can be taken as typical:

April 3. *French brig loaded with wine prize to the Brilliant lugger arrived.*

April 4. *French sloop loaded with wine prize to the Brilliant arrived.*

April 16. *Tartar privateer arrived with his prize ship Indispensable (500 tons) with sugar from San Domingo, also French L'Aimable Victoire from Bayonne with 800 barrels of flour prize to the Brilliant.*

April 25. *Brilliant privateer arrived with a French lugsail privateer, Le Malouin, of 6 guns and 25 men his prize.*

April 26. *Sprightly privateer arrived with a French cutter privateer, Le Republican, of 8 guns and 40 men, his prize.*

April 29. *Resolution privateer arrived with his prize ship L'Heureux of Bordeaux of 400 tons, from Charleston with rice, tobacco and timber.*

A little later he recorded news of Captain Saumarez, the island's naval hero. 'News of the Crescent frigate having captured La Réunion, French frigate of 36 guns off Cherbourg last Sunday.' There was great rejoicing over this as the *Crescent* carried an almost completely Guernsey crew.

Yet these naval adventures did not always end successfully, as William Mooney, an English visitor in 1798, recorded in his Diary: 'One little square-set being engaged our attention. His name is Queripel. In the last war he commanded a small schooner privateer of 2 Tons, called the Hat and Wig, the joint property of Mr. Touzel, the Hatter, and Rabey, a Barber. He sailed from this port on a cruize in the Bay of Biscay, where he had not been long before he fell in with a large French ship L'Argonaut of 700 tons burden, bound to Bordeaux. Having hoisted his colours he gave the Frenchman the broadside of his swivels.' The end of the story was ignominious. As Queripel and his crew of eight boarded the French ship, they were seized and put in the hold and the Hat and Wig was hoisted on board L'Argonaut.

Mr. Mooney was also witness to the extent of the legitimate entrepôt trade, as well as to the smuggling which continued unchecked. He recorded: 'Guernsey is the Emporium of a Universal Trade, and in 1796–7 the Exports from hence to England paid one million and a half into the Customs and Excise. This island is most conveniently situated for commerce with every part of Europe, and from its proximity to French ports, its merchants are enabled to take advantage of the state of their markets, as no others can.'

He also remarked: 'From a window we observed a smuggler taking in his cargo of spirits and tobacco for the coast of Sussex.' It followed inevitably that as the English Government extended the range and raised the charges on dutiable articles to get money for the war, so that by 1797 some 1,200 articles were taxed, the smugglers found their business more and more profitable, and this benefited the island middlemen. The Bailiff of Guernsey and two of the jurats admitted that in the last quarter of 1800 they had exported 3,325 pipes and 983 hogsheads of brandy and wine.

After the brief respite of the Treaty of Amiens, the war flared up again, with Great Britain facing the full power of the Napoleonic Empire. The threat to the Islands was increased. Napoleon fulminated against them, especially Jersey, 'France can no longer tolerate this nest of brigands and assassins. Europe must be purged. Jersey is England's shame.'

The English Government made very adequate preparations. They appointed two able Lieutenant-Governors, General Don and General Sir John Doyle. General Don pushed ahead the fortification of the Town Hill above St. Helier with the construction of Fort Regent, and he took other wise measures. He organized a system of signals, by which, if a French fleet left St. Malo, the news could pass via look-out ships to Mont Orgueil and on to Grosnez, to Sark and to the British squadron in St. Peter Port, in a quarter of an hour. He also greatly improved the Jersey roads, in spite of some opposition. His first road, from the town to Grouville, was held up by an old farmer who threatened to shoot the first man who dug a sod. So the General, in full regimentals, took a spade and dug through the boundary bank. The farmer did not shoot.

Similar improvements were made to Guernsey's road system by General Doyle, who had studied the first Ordnance Survey map of the island, and quickly realized the primitive nature of the communications. He drove two new roads through the island, from the town to Vazon, and from the town to L'Erée. The money to pay for this big scheme he raised by a most far-sighted enterprise.

He had realized that the Clos du Valle, the north-east corner, was almost completely isolated by the sea, and, if seized by the enemy, could be a dangerous stronghold. So he carried through the draining of the sea inlet, and thus linked the area safely with the rest of Guernsey, while at the same time he reclaimed about 300 acres. The money from the sale of this land was enough to pay for the road construction.

During this emergency the garrison was increased to 4,000 infantry and a company of artillery, and extra barracks were built to house them at points along the north-west coast. The militia, too, were intensively trained and breastworks were built all along the coastline, with batteries covering every bay.

To make assurance doubly sure the British squadron

based on St. Peter Port was placed under the command of James Saumarez, now an Admiral after his distinguished service at Cape St. Vincent, Algeciras, and the Nile. His task, which he carried out to the letter, was to blockade a French fleet in Brest; by this he ensured that Admiral Villeneuve was not at full strength when he finally met Nelson at Trafalgar. Admiral Saumarez also destroyed a flotilla of gunboats which were due to sail from Granville to Boulogne, the great invasion assembly point.

Even before Trafalgar the scheme of invasion was dead, an immense relief to Great Britain and to the Islands. Yet they were hard hit by the imposition of Napoleon's 'Continental System', which officially closed the ports of all western Europe to British trade. Britain's reply hit them hard too. By an act of 1807 the English Smuggling Act was extended to cover the seas around the Islands, and was enforced by the establishment of Customs departments. The merchants of both islands accepted the situation with as good a grace as they could, and Guernsey followed Jersey's example, establishing a Chamber of Commerce to stop illicit traffic. For a time the more adventurous merchants transferred their business to Alderney, but eventually the Customs officers got some control of that island too. Smuggling then became the resort of small men, hiding tobacco or a few kegs in caves for their customers to collect on dark nights. One of these hide-outs was the Creux-Mahie in Guernsey, a cavern 260 feet long and 40 feet high, which is reputed to have been connected by an underground passage to St. Saviour's Church, two miles away. Another was a Wesleyan chapel, where fishermen who crept up to investigate a light shining from a window claimed to have seen the Devil, with horns and tail, and fire belching from his mouth. It was left undecided whether the reality was the Devil or an ingenious invention to deter the curious.

Smuggling might be severely checked, privateering no longer so paying owing to the scarcity of prizes, the entrepôt trade be diminished by the setting up of bonded warehouses in Britain, but, while the war continued, there were other opportunities for enterprise. The campaign in the Spanish Peninsula opened up the ports of Spain and her rebellious overseas empire to the island shippers and merchants. A dangerous but lucrative triangular trade developed, as the bold merchants carried codfish from Newfoundland to Spain; from there they carried wine and brandy to Rio de Janeiro or the River Plate, and from those ports they brought back home sugar, coffee, and hides. A brig could clear upwards of £9,000 on one voyage on this route.

A second opening arose when Napoleon relaxed the trade embargo of his 'Continental System', and allowed traffic in certain goods. Guernsey became the principal market-place for their interchange, and, in spite of many difficulties and restrictions as the enemy governments varied their policies, the merchants made useful profits.

The Peninsular War had another helpful effect on Guernsey with its big roadstead. St. Peter Port became the staging camp, the half-way house, for regiments in transit to and from Lisbon, and all these troops were extra customers for the merchants, shopkeepers, farmers and peasants of the island.

In 1812 the privateers suddenly found themselves with a new target, American shipping. The quarrel between Great Britain and the United States arose over the continental blockade and the searching of American vessels for Royal Navy deserters. But to the islanders this war meant valuable prizes. One American vessel alone, which was caught on her way from Calcutta, was worth £60,000.

The American War also meant the triumph and death of Major-General Sir Isaac Brock, a Guernseyman, who after many years of able and devoted professional service in the Army, was then acting as both Governor and General in Upper Canada. Although he was supposed to be holding a frontier of 1,300 miles with scarcely as many men, he took the offensive and marched to capture Detroit. This success united behind him the Anglo-Saxons and the French

Canadians, and won him the support of the six Indian nations. Although he was killed in a skirmish two months later, his example had inspired his people to resist a more powerful American offensive in the following year, and there is no doubt that it was his energy and inspiration which saved Canada for Britain.

At last, on 27th June 1814, Elisha Dobrée noted in his Diary: 'Peace proclaimed. Town illuminated.' Except for the Hundred Days, the long war with France was over. Though there was general rejoicing, the French Wars had brought considerable prosperity to all the islands, and particularly to Guernsey. There had been provided great opportunities for the enterprising merchant and sea captain, steady markets for the farmer, steady employment for the craftsman and labourer. The presence of large garrisons and of naval officers had brought money to the Islands, and had also stimulated social life. The sudden transition back to peacetime was bound to present difficulties, but also new challenges.

Chapter 10

An Age of Some Enterprise, 1815—1914

VICTOR HUGO wrote a significant description of the Guernsey people in his day: that 'they consisted of those who were content to ramble round their gardens and those who were content to ramble round the world.' This shrewd summary was shown to be true of the peoples of all the Islands in the nineteenth century, though of course the proportion of stay-at-homes and adventurers varied from period to period.

One of the first of the adventurers of this time was Thomas de la Rue, a young man of Huguenot descent, from the Forest parish in Guernsey. He had served his apprenticeship and worked on the staff of a number of island printing firms, including that which published the first Guernsey newspaper, the *Gazette de L'ile de Guernesey*, started in 1789. In his time all the newspapers were in French, and his comment on them, 'C'est trop peut-être pour cette isle,' may have prompted the foundation of the first English language paper, the Star, in 1813. De la Rue himself grew dissatisfied with his prospects in the island by 1816, and crossed by cutter to England, to seek his fortune in London. There he used his skills first in the manufacture of straw hats, but soon returned to printing, especially to the production of high-class playing cards. His firm went from strength to strength, and soon he won as world-wide a reputation for his products as the Jerseyman, Martel, was winning for his.

Such was one young islander's adjustment to the post-war

situation. But a considerable proportion of the populations of all the Islands, especially the country people, were conservative, suspicious of change, and of strangers. How would they react to the challenges, needs and new influences of a century in which life seemed to many to be too busy?

After the end of the war, which closed the period of privateering, and saw a great reduction in smuggling and the withdrawal of a large proportion of the garrisons, there was a considerable depression, and a possibility that the Islands would relapse into rural backwaters, cut off by their patois and poor communications from the vigorous country to the north and destined to be depressed and depopulated areas, much as is the case today with Belle Isle, a very similar island off the French Biscay coast.

Yet there were a number of factors which enabled the Islands to escape such a fate. First, although the English garrisons were much reduced, the Islands were still regarded as fortresses by the English Government. It is true that the threat from the traditional enemy, France, was much less, but for most of the century the English Government was faced by rivalry from across the Channel. The garrisons of the two Bailiwicks were kept at a regular battalion and a company of Field and Coastal Artillery each. In Jersey this force was based on Fort Regent, with detachments in the other forts round the coast. The battalion allotted to Guernsey was split, half being stationed in the island forts and half in Alderney. The gunners manned their guns in Castle Cornet and Clarence Battery, and in Fort George where heavy coastal guns were trained permanently on the Russel passage.

The presence of these regular garrisons, among which were numbered during the years some of the most famous British regiments, not only served to give the islanders a greater sense of security and to help their economies by the money they brought in and the civilian jobs they provided, they also acted as quickeners of the islanders' pulse, the officers mingling with and leavening the island gentry, the men challenging and stirring the islanders' pride and patriotism by their military swagger and their turn-out on parade. Not that the regular soldiers were always popular; many a private was glad to escape to the safety of the Picquet House, the Town Guard House, after a rough night in the town, and many a respectable island householder trembled as he listened to the Irish or the Highlanders making their way back to barracks on a Saturday night. But the citizens were always conscious of them, whether it was the daily gun signal at noon and 9.30 p.m. from the castle, the weekly church parade when the men marched, later in the century, from Fort George to the garrison church of St. James the Less, the Sunday military band concert, or the great occasion of the year, the Sovereign's Birthday, La Grande Mourtre.

On this occasion the regular garrisons and the island militias were seen on parade together. From an early hour the islanders flocked in from all the parishes to the parade ground. 'Es'che pour la Reine?' ('Are you to the Queen's Parade?') was heard on all sides. There the regulars were drawn up for inspection and on the same parade ground the regiments of the militia, from 1831 known as the Royal Jersey and the Royal Guernsey. After a full inspection by the Lieutenant-Governor and his staff, the ceremonial trooping of the colour and the march past, a gun sounded from the fort at noon, and twenty more guns followed it to mark the end of the ceremony. The day was not ended; a fun fair, music by the band and fireworks sustained the excitement until late at night.

The island militias, marching so proudly on parade that day, remained a vital contribution to the English conception of the Islands as fortresses, and a formidable argument that the Islands should not be ignored. Although they were reorganized periodically during the century, and their numbers were cut down, the older men between forty-five and sixty being posted to a reserve, they were undoubtedly a useful force. Their standards of efficiency and drill were maintained by weekly practice, and in the nineteen hundreds by camp training, and their loyalty and readiness were unquestioned. There is only one record of trouble. The regular adjutant appointed to the North Regiment was a Captain Pym, a tactless man who did not appreciate the difference between regular soldiers and the tough quarrymen and labourers who had turned out for parade after a hard day's work. His attitude and language upset them and opposition mounted until one day only one man turned up for parade. The Royal Court was responsible for the final enforcement of military discipline, and sentenced the ringleaders to a month's solitary confinement. When the condemned men were released, there was a large popular demonstration, and they marched back from the gaol to St. Sampson's in a triumphal procession. With the departure of the unpopular adjutant all was smoothed over, but he was not forgotten. 'Pas Pour Pym' was a family saying in the northern Guernsey parishes for some generations.

The island whose fortunes were most affected by the garrison conception was Alderney. There the declaration of peace, with the end to privateering and the curb on smuggling, caused great distress. This rebounded on the head of the hereditary Governor, John le Mesurier, who had succeeded in 1803. He had already been in trouble during the war, as his position as commander of the Alderney Militia carried little weight with the regular officers of the garrison, and his claim to the title of Seigneur annoyed the Alderney jurats. Some of the Alderney people had the courage to escape from their poverty to the United States, but many stayed, restless and dissatisfied with the fall in their living standards. Le Mesurier found that his reources were not sufficient to remedy the situation, and, with the disillusioned comment, 'These men, the sons of Zeruiah, be too hard for me,' he applied to the British Government in 1825 for his patent to be revoked in return for compensation.

Little was altered by his departure. The civil power was vested in the Court, presided over by the Judge, who was assisted by six elected jurats. Yet they could not find any immediate cure for the distress, now aggravated by the fact that the Governor's household was no more. At last, in 1830, when the population had sunk to a thousand, it was agreed to divide the common lands among the fifty-two island-born families. These lands, assessed as Good and Poor, were distributed by lot, each family receiving one Good and one Poor portion. With this accession of property the surviving families settled down for the time to farm the island as they had done before the lure of easier wealth had tempted them.

The Alderney scene was materially transformed some ten years later. The Admiralty were alarmed by the growth of a strongly fortified naval base at Cherbourg and planned to make Alderney into 'The Gibraltar of the Channel'. Their scheme was a grandiose one, to construct a harbour of refuge and observation at Braye Bay, and a great breakwater, some 4,680 feet long, was begun in 1847. Unfortunately the original plan, to build it on the foundation of a line of rocks, was abandoned, and the new plan involved laying the foundations in twenty fathoms of sea. This exposed the man-made masonry to the full force of the storms. The stone for this was quarried locally, and for this work and the building of the breakwater and the chain of ten forts from Fort Clonque to Fort Essex, which rose up to guard the less defensible coast of the island, a large labour force, mostly Irish, was brought in. By 1860 the population had risen to nearly 5,000.

The Alderney people benefited from the vast expenditure on this project, some one and a half million pounds, and from the employment in building the breakwater, forts and houses for the workers. Yet the whole scheme was of very dubious value, both to the Admiralty and to the island. Only six months after the completion of the breakwater in 1864, the winter gales tore two huge breaches in the wall and the cost of this repair, added to the excessive original cost, appalled the English Treasury.

For a time it was touch and go whether the breakwater

would be abandoned, but the islanders' plea that it had ruined their original anchorage was listened to. With great difficulty the breakwater was kept in repair till the end of the century. Then changing needs and the development in the range of coastal artillery from France rendered the plan even more obsolete, and it was decided to abandon roughly half of the breakwater. The abandoned section became a sunken reef, which made the approach to the harbour dangerous.

Even less successful was the companion Admiralty scheme for Jersey. This envisaged a great harbour for the fleet in St. Catherine's Bay. Eight hundred workmen were brought over, and one arm of the breakwater was built. However the expense, and hints from France that it was looked on as an unnecessarily unfriendly act, changed the English Government's mind. The second breakwater was never started, and eventually the long white elephant was handed over to the Jersey States.

Another source of friction with the French at this time was the presence in the Islands of French Republican exiles. After the series of unsuccessful revolutions on the Continent in 1848, many republicans and Socialists fled to Jersey. Among Les Proscrits, as those fleeing from Louis Napoleon were called, was Victor Hugo. Some of these exiles had little to do except to meet and plot and protest, and the French among them produced a paper, *L'Homme*, which expressed violent disapproval of the visit of Queen Victoria to Napoleon III. The Jerseymen were naturally very indignant, the paper was burnt, and the three editors were expelled by the Governor. When Victor Hugo protested at this treatment, he was driven out too, and crossed over to Guernsey.

There he settled down happily for fifteen years, buying Hauteville House which he decorated and furnished to his taste. He could look out over the harbour and the Islands from his study in the attic, and there he wrote much of his poetry and three of his most famous novels. Some of the action of one of these, *The Toilers of the Sea*, was set in the area of Bordeaux Harbour, and he showed his affection for Guernsey by its dedication—'Au rocher d'hospitalité et de liberté, à ce coin de vieille terre Normande, à l'ile de Guernsey'.

With the emergence of the Republic in 1870, tension between France and England relaxed in the Channel Isles area, the only remaining source of trouble being disputes over fishing rights. These led in 1883 to an attempt by the French to take over the rocky islets of the Ecrehos. There they came up against the stout resistance of Philip Pinel, a Jerseyman who lived a solitary life there for forty years or so, mainly to escape from his wife who lived at Rozel. The French claim failed, as did a later one in the twentieth century to the dangerous Minquiers, south of St. Helier.

It was the deep consciousness of their *liberté*, of the ancient charters and privileges on which the Islands' survival as entities was based, which was the second helpful factor in this period. Although intensely loyal, the islanders naturally set great store by their independence and resisted grimly and stubbornly all attempts by English ministers to override these rights, and all attempts by the English Parliament to interfere. On the whole the English Government, aided by wise advice from the Lieutenant-Governors, handled the island governments sympathetically, but there were a number of critical occasions.

The leading figure in early protests was Daniel de Lisle Brock, Bailiff of Guernsey from 1821 and a brother of Sir Isaac. He had already in the war had experience as the advocate for Channel Isles privileges, when, as a jurat, he was sent to London to protest before the Privy Council against Admiralty attempts to impress men for the Navy. Supported by the expert opinion of Lord Saumarez, he had carried the day against Lord St. Vincent.

On Brock's appointment as bailiff, he found himself battling against the application of an English Act which prohibited the entry of foreign corn into the Channel Isles whenever its import into Britain was forbidden. This was clearly contrary to the Islands' claim to be free ports.

Some ten years later the export of corn from the Islands caused another crisis. Plymouth merchants accused the islanders of bringing into England much greater quantities of corn than they could possibly grow themselves. Customs officers followed up by demanding duty on it. To meet this challenge to the Islands' rights and to a valuable trade, Brock led a deputation from Guernsey and Jersey which successfully proved that the accusations were false, and made clear the nature of the Islands' duty rights.

In 1832 he defended another vital principle, that of islanders only being tried in their own courts. A St. Pancras beadle was arrested in Guernsey for dumping paupers on the island. When the St. Pancras Council, backed by the English Courts, attempted to extricate him by applying the Habeas Corpus Act, the deputy sheriff resisted the interference. St. Pancras then went further, and sent a warrant for the trial of the deputy sheriff in England. An island embassy, led by Brock, went to London to make a successful protest.

Brock died in 1843. His experience, wisdom and tact were to be greatly missed when the next struggle occurred. The new Lieutenant-Governor was Major-General Sir William Napier, a man famous for his active career in the Peninsular War, and especially as the author of *The Peninsular War*, a book which had set new standards in military history. The more progressive islanders had great hopes of him, as he had the reputation of a liberal reformer as well as of one with a lively and original mind. But his period of office came near to disaster, for he apparently failed completely to understand the position of the bailiff and the jurats and thought of them as ignorant civilians, whose local powers could be easily overriden by his military authority and prestige as the Queen's representative.

Soon after his arrival he had the first clash, when he expelled a Frenchman from the island on his own authority.

This led to a tense interview between Napier and the bailiff, made even tenser by Napier's refusal to discuss anything with the bailiff while the jurats were present. The situation simmered for a time, and then Napier issued a free pardon to a soldier whom the Royal Court had sent to prison for assault. This action of his was contrary to island law. A petition to the Queen followed, which the Home Secretary, Sir James Graham, dealt with inconclusively. Indignation in the island grew, and Napier was certainly unpopular. Yet the next move amazed everyone. In May 1844 a force of 600 men was landed at St. Peter Port from troop transports 'to quell the island's insurrection'. The island leaders learnt that there was talk of 'an alleged conspiracy to poison or shoot the Lieutenant-Governor'.

A great protest meeting was held on the New Ground. There gathered between twelve and thirteen thousand angry and offended citizens, to consider the statement that 'imputations had been recently thrown upon the loyalty of the inhabitants of the island'. The venerable General Sir Thomas Saumarez was chosen to carry a loyal address across the sea to the Queen, and the Home Secretary had to cover up the gaffe as best he could. Yet Napier remained as Lieutenant-Governor.

In 1846 Queen Victoria herself, with Prince Albert, took a hand in the struggle. On the suggestion of Sir George Grey, the new Whig Home Secretary, who was himself the grandson of a former Lieutenant-Governor, she paid a surprise visit to the island. Fog held up her voyage from Plymouth, but she eventually arrived off St. Peter Port in the evening. Not deigning to receive Napier on her yacht, she intimated that she would land and drive on a small tour the next morning. Everyone worked busily for most of the night, and next day she landed, to be received by a bevy of local beauties in white, and by the cheers of the garrison, militia and citizens on her whole route. It was reported that the enthusiastic militiamen held their arms at the present in their left hands and waved their shakos with their right.

After a triumphantly loyal reception she re-embarked, to sail on to Jersey, where similar delirious crowds received her. Landing at the new south pier, which was promptly renamed the Victoria Pier, she drove to Mont Orgueil and then back to her yacht.

It was a great occasion for both islands, the first time they had been visited by the reigning sovereign. The visit was commemorated in Guernsey by the construction of the Victoria Tower, on the site of an old mill above the town, and in Jersey by the decision to build a college, to be named Victoria College when the foundation-stone was laid four years later.

In spite of this demonstration Napier remained as Lieutenant-Governor of Guernsey for another year, initiating further rows, especially over his abrupt dismissal of some militia officers. One of these was Lieut.-Colonel Tupper, of a notable service family, who had lost eleven relatives on active service. Under island law he and the others were liable to serve as privates when they lost their commissions, but it was arranged that Tupper should be excused on the grounds that the uniforms were too small for him while Napier remained as Commander-in-Chief.

At last Sir George Grey, who found Napier's rudeness intolerable, persuaded the Duke of Wellington to replace him, and a new Lieutenant-Governor arrived, General Bell, who by his kindness and courtesy was destined to heal the wounds.

Yet this fracas was one reason for the English Government's looking with a critical eye at the island Constitutions. It was natural, especially after the Reform Bill of 1832, that the climate of opinion in England should not be too favourable to what appeared on the surface to be oligarchic governments claiming excessive independence. No doubt the adverse comments of General Napier helped to add to the impression. A further stimulus came from Jersey.

In Jersey after the peace the political struggle between the Progressives, who took the rose for their emblem, and the

Conservatives, who chose a laurel leaf, broke out again. The *New Guide to Jersey* reported: 'The natives are divided into two factions, the Laurel and the Rose, who hate each other more bitterly than rival actors and singers. They seldom inter-visit, seldom inter-marry, seldom salute each other in the streets, and they carry their animosities into every transaction of their lives, legislative, judicial, municipal, and private.'

Into this cockpit poured English visitors, some of them for a holiday, but a fair proportion to settle in the island. They were attracted by the climate, by the improved communications, for steamers started running from Southampton, Portsmouth and Plymouth in the twenties, and by the low cost of living. This particularly appealed to those officers who retired on half pay after the war. They found that many articles were untaxed which were liable to tax in England, that unless they bought real property they were not liable to pay poor rates or parish rates, and that the rate of exchange between English currency and island currency favoured them.

The currencies of both Jersey and Guernsey had reached a chaotic condition by the end of the war, and both island governments had issued new ones, Guernsey in 1829, Jersey in 1834. Among the Guernsey copper currency of liards or doubles had been found old English farthings, Dutch, Flemish, French and Spanish coins, thin pieces of plain copper and even soldier's buttons beaten flat. All these were withdrawn and a new currency of francs and doubles was introduced, at the rate of eight doubles to the penny and two hundred and fifty-two pennies to the pound. The less conservative Jerseymen adopted pounds, shillings and pence, linking this currency with their old established coins by making a halfpenny equal in value to a sou, with five hundred and twenty sous to a pound.

Thus the half-pay officer received slightly more for his pension in Jersey, and though some settled in Guernsey, the majority chose the rival island. By 1840 there were 15,000 English residents, mainly settled in new streets which grew up on the outskirts of St. Helier. These people tended to live as an English colony, with their own churches or chapels, their own newspapers, and their own social life. They rarely mixed with the Jerseymen—one commentator wrote: 'One thing very striking in Jersey is the extraordinary contrast between business and idleness. The English have nothing to do. The object of one part of the population is to get quit of time, while the object of the native inhabitants is to make the most of it.'

The more inquiring, or the more peppery, among this group found the Jersey system of government largely incomprehensible, and the local laws even more so. They backed a campaign, which was led by a Jerseyman, Abraham Le Cras, to prove that Jersey had no right to govern herself, and that the Jersey States had only the powers of a Municipal Council. According to Le Cras: 'The States have no more power to make laws for Jersey than I have.' Improperly, but unsuccessfully, he tried to stir English M.P.s into interfering, but he did succeed in securing the appointment of a Royal Commission to inquire into the state of the Criminal Law in the Islands.

This Commission found the need for radical changes in Jersey, largely because the jurats, who were party men, Rose or Laurel, were also the justices. It therefore proposed to abolish the Royal Court and to replace it by three Crown-appointed judges, and to form a paid police force.

When it looked at Guernsey it found an even more horrifying situation. It reported: 'According to the theory of the Guernsey constitution, the Jurats may on one day, sitting in the Court of Chief Pleas, make an Ordonnance without the consent of Your Majesty, against the will of the functionary representing the Crown in the island, and without consulting the body of the States, and on the next day, sitting as a Court of Justice, they may proceed to put their own construction on it and to execute the law of their own making, without their decision in any matter of criminal law being capable of review by any superior authority.' Yet the Commission had to admit, to their own surprise, that powers so unlimited appeared to be little abused.

For the moment the result of the Commission was virtually nil. It is true that the Guernsey leaders paid lip-service to the idea of democracy by releasing the constables of the parishes from their duty to attend the States of Deliberation, and by replacing them with delegates from the Parish Douzaines; but they made no further move until the end of the century, when for the first time twelve People's Deputies were elected on a limited franchise to sit in the States. The fact was that the people of Guernsey were quite happy with the situation as it was. Except for a few grumbles from the commercial classes at the cautious attitude of their leaders, there was no party feeling, and even the social rivalry of the two cliques, of the Sixties and the Forties, died down. With changing social ideas the Assembly Rooms, that bone of contention, fell out of use, and after being bought by the States for public entertainments such as hypnotism by Mesmer, and performances by Chirgwin, 'the white-eyed Kaffir', the rooms were converted by Guille and Allés in 1882 into a Public Library and Museum.

In Jersey, too, where the dominant party of the Laurels was led by the lawyer Advocate Godfrey, no action was taken. Yet the earlier agitation by Le Cras was not forgotten by the Privy Council, nor was the Commission's Report. In 1852 the Council issued three Orders, establishing a Police Court, a Petty Debts Court, and a paid Police Force for the town. This attack on the island's right of self-government united Advocate Godfrey and his deadly rival, Advocate Le Sueur, and their supporters, and a petition signed by 7,000 people was sent, asking for the Orders to be withdrawn. At last a compromise was reached—the Orders were withdrawn, and the States themselves passed virtually the same measures. They also bowed to outside pressure so far as to add fourteen elected deputies to the traditional components of the States, the Jurats, the Rectors, and the Constables.

Even then Le Cras and his supporters were not satisfied. Again they agitated and lobbied M.P.s, and a second Royal Commission was set up, which recommended the appointment by the Crown of paid judges. The Jerseymen ignored the recommendation. So Le Cras stirred his friends in the English Parliament to bring forward a Bill, 'to amend the Constitution of Jersey'. At one time this Bill reached the committee stage. But the island leaders countered with a plebiscite, in which they asked the citizens to vote on the simple alternative, 'Jurats or Paid Judges'. The vote for the ancient office of jurat was almost unanimous, and at last Le Cras abandoned the struggle.

The Islands' status as fortresses with garrisons and their stubborn struggles to live, trade, be governed and tried in their own way undoubtedly contributed to their continued strength and vitality in this century. The most fundamental factors in their survival however were those two qualities of the Victorian era, private enterprise and public spirit.

In both Jersey and Guernsey the lead in improving the amenities for the people and in providing public buildings of dignity had been taken by private citizens in the middle of the eighteenth century. Both islands had been provided with an hôpital, a building which acted as infirmary, workhouse and orphanage. Generous endowments were made to support the hospital authorities in their care of the poor, in particular in Guernsey by the Perchard banking family, one of whose members rose to be Lord Mayor of London. Another benefactor of Jersey had been the island historian, Falle, who had founded and stocked a public library near Royal Square as early as 1736.

It was some time before the States of either island felt impelled to take action themselves, and by the end of the eighteenth century their only positive achievements had been, in Jersey, the building of a new breakwater for St. Helier harbour and the improvement of the Royal Court buildings. In Guernsey a fine new granite Court House was built in 1799 at the top of Smith Street, to form the centre of a new administrative and legal area. The money for this building was raised half from harbour dues and half from a public lottery.

It was the shortage of public funds and the uncertain situation in the Napoleonic War which postponed further action. Yet the Guernsey authorities were well aware that their Old Town was virtually unchanged since medieval times, that it was crowded, congested and squalid, even if picturesque. Fresh impetus was given to improvements by the ending of the war and by a ruling of the Privy Council that the parishioners of St. Peter Port were not liable to raise money for new buildings. The States were forced to look elsewhere for an increase in public funds, and found it in a duty on imported wines and spirits.

With this income and a large labour force available as a result of post-war unemployment, a considerable rebuilding programme was undertaken, which did much to change the appearance and layout of the Old Town. Streets in which the occupants of the top storeys had been able to shake hands with their opposite numbers, were widened, given underground drains and paved. The exits from the town were improved so that it was possible for carts to meet and pass. Covered Fish and Meat Markets were built, with the latest improvements such as marble slabs for the fish and a supply of running water. The financing of the cost of the fine Meat Markets was most ingenious; some £4,000 was raised by the issue of non-interest-bearing notes, which were destroyed as the income to redeem them came in from stallholders.

The impetus towards another improvement came from a Jerseyman, Le Boutellier, who had taken up business in Guernsey. He was extremely critical of the standard of education in the island, particularly of Elizabeth College, and in 1821 he forwarded proposals to the new Lieutenant-Governor, Sir John Colborne. He was an able and sympathetic man, who loved the island and who, when later he was appointed Governor of Upper Canada, nostalgically renamed the township of the Rapids Sarnia. His favourable influence and that of Bailiff Brock led to the appointment of a committee which discovered that much of the land bequeathed by Queen Elizabeth had been alienated at some time or other, that at the time there were only sixteen pupils and that there had never been more than twenty-five, and that the master, the Rev. N. Carey, felt no obligation to teach anybody anything. After some difficulty Carey was induced to resign, and a new principal, Dr. Stocker, famed for his flogging powers, was appointed. A new constitution was drawn up for the school and funds were voted for the erection of a new building. For this the promoters engaged as architect John Wilson, the designer of other Guernsey buildings such as Castle Carey and the Church of St. James the Less.

This church had been built, under the patronage of Lord Saumarez, to fill the need for an Anglican service in English for the new English residents and for the upper strata of Guernsey society who were becoming more and more anglicized. No doubt it was the influence of Lord Saumarez, now at the peak of his career as Vice-Admiral of England, which led to the arrival of the Bishop of Salisbury in a 46-gun frigate to consecrate the church in 1818.

Le Boutellier's enterprise was not confined to reform of the college. Besides introducing gas to the island he set on foot a most ambitious project, to remove some narrow alleys and quarry away thousands of tons from the side of Mont Gibel, at the back of High Street, and there to build a new Commerical Arcade, with four entrances and a glass roof. The cost of this scheme bankrupted him before it was finished, but the final result was a pedestrian shopping precinct which modern planners may envy.

While the Old Town was thus being changed the families who had made fortunes out of privateering were extending the town outwards up the valleys and on the hills above. There in the new town of Clifton, up the Grange, in higher Hauteville and in the very select area of Cambridge Park a large number of new mansions or terraces were built, in late Georgian or Regency style, to provide their owners with comfortable and elegant homes, and to add to the vista of St. Peter Port from the sea.

By about 1830 the building urge had somewhat subsided, but fresh impetus was given to town improvements by an outbreak of cholera. The emergency was tackled by the burning of tar and attempted fumigation; yet the real cure lay in further opening up of the town's narrow streets and alleys, and over the years this was done.

Although this cholera outbreak caused more deaths in Jersey, the incidence was not concentrated in one area, and the authorities had not the same necessity to redevelop. They built good markets in St. Helier, but their main concern was the provision of an adequate harbour. In 1817, when the Duke of Gloucester paid a visit, he had to scramble ashore over the rocks, and later Prince Albert asked why the islanders had their harbour on dry land. The difficulty arose from the great rise and fall of the tide—40 feet at times. A cargo quay was built, an esplanade over the dunes to provide an approach from the land, and in 1837 James Walker was commissioned to plan a new harbour, consisting of what came to be called the Victoria and Albert Piers, for which he used local stone from the great Mont Mado quarry. Even then the problem of a tidal harbour, exposed to the Atlantic gales, was not solved. Later a most ambitious project, which would have incorporated Elizabeth Castle in a great outer breakwater, had to be abandoned, with heavy losses, and the Jersey States were forced to fall back on dredging their existing basin.

The need for a large deep-water harbour also faced the Guernsey States. They had the old harbour, now filled to bursting with shipping, and during these years they improved the shoreline on either side, building esplanades to north and south. They were also spending large sums on improvements to the basin at St. Sampson's. Yet the old harbour and St. Sampson's were both tidal, a most inconvenient situation for the steamers and steam packets which increasingly brought passengers, cargo and mail from English ports. The bailiff, Brock, was favourable to new proposals, pressure from commercial firms increased, but for the time the Guernsey Court and States would make no move.

At last, in 1851, inspired by a forward-looking jurat, Henry Tupper, approval was given to a great plan prepared by a well-known engineer, Rendel. Work started in 1853, and gradually over the years the encircling breakwaters were finished and the quays built. The cost, £360,000, was a heavy one for a small community, but instead of a harbour of four acres, the Guernsey people found themselves with one of eighty acres, and the resulting benefit to the island's communications, trade and prosperity was almost immeasurable.

Jurat Tupper's drive and vision brought other improvements. A postal service, maintained by two Government sailing packets, had been started, on the order of the English Government, in 1794, as a necessity in time of war. Gradually improvements had been made, and faced with competition from privately owned steamers running from Southampton, the Post Office went over to steam, running twice weekly from Weymouth. Later reorganization led to a delivery on six days a week. Even so there were delays, so that it was a great day for the islanders when, on the 7th September 1858, a telegraph service via submarine cable was opened between the island and England. A message on that day was delivered in the City of London in forty minutes, and Henry Tupper and the other company directors could well feel proud.

Tupper's other outstanding success was the agreement to build Les Hanois lighthouse on the dangerous rocks off Guernsey's western promontory. There had been a light in the Channel Isles area since 1723; this was on the Casquet Rocks, which rise abruptly some 113 feet out of the sea to the west of Alderney. Yet in spite of many wrecks, including that of H.M.S. *Boreas* with the loss of 127 lives in 1807, nothing was done to mark Les Hanois and to provide a guide for navigation for the many ships which were swept off course by the great indraught of tide into the Bay of Avranches. For many years the battle went on between the bailiff, Sir Stafford Carey, backed by the Chamber of Commerce, and Trinity House, mainly on the question of who was to pay for the light. At last, in 1860, influenced by Tupper's arguments, Trinity House gave way, and work started on the dangerous job of building the 100-foot lighthouse. Some ten years later the second dangerous westerly point, La Corbière, off Jersey, was equipped with a lighthouse too.

The last and most vital factor in the story of the Islands in this century, on which their survival mainly depended, was of course the enterprise of the individual islanders, the degree to which they were able to use their skills, resources and geographical position to earn a living.

Immediately after the war in 1815 the Jerseymen had an advantage in that their economy had grown more naturally. The farmers, with their farms of a more economic size than in Guernsey, continued on their more or less traditional way, growing wheat and barley and cider apples, and, influenced by the advice and example of Colonel le Couteur, breeding better cattle. A considerable export trade in Jersey bulls, cows and calves was built up to England and the United States, averaging some hundreds of beasts a year. The other main export crop was that of autumn-dug potatoes.

This remained the pattern of Jersey agriculture until 1880. In that year a farmer, Hugh de la Haye, was holding his annual Grande Charrue party to celebrate the deep ploughing, and passed round two huge potatoes, one with sixteen eyes. The guests cut them into pieces at the table, and the next day the bits were planted. In the spring of 1881 a large early crop appeared, and Farmer de la Haye, realizing the possibilities, built up his stock carefully. He named it the Royal Jersey Fluke. From this developed the early potato export trade, which in ten years had risen to 70,000 tons and had brought in nearly a half million pounds to the growers.

The other traditional industry was the Newfoundland cod trade, which revived and expanded after the war. As the years passed the emphasis changed. Jersey firms, such as Charles Robin and Co. owned the Canadian and Newfoundland fishing stations, but more and more became the middlemen, the merchants. They ran mixed cargoes of stores, clothing, boots and shoes out to the stations, took the salt cod to South America or Spain, and returned to Jersey with hides, wine and other goods. The degree to which the fisheries depended on Jersey finance and control can be gauged from the fact that when, after a series of private bank failures, the Jersey Bank, the biggest, crashed in 1886, there were riots among the Canadian fishermen, clamouring for the money which could not be paid.

To supply the sailing ships for this trade a considerable shipbuilding industry grew up and the yards stretched round the coast from St. Aubin's right to St. Catherine's. In the first fifty years of the period the tonnage of Jersey shipping rose from 9,000 tons to 50,000 tons, and the number of trading ships to 450. Gradually the competition from iron or steel-built ships ousted these schooners and cutters and the yards were forced to close, a fate which was in store for the industry in Guernsey too.

In the early years another development was the expansion of the oyster beds off Gorey. These had been fished locally for some time, but then English firms discovered the beds and sent over about three hundred boats to join in the dredging. The catches were sorted and packed by women and girls at Gorey. Unhappily the English exploited the beds too greedily, and trouble flared up with the French and with the island authorities. First the French objected when the English boats moved in to dredge their beds off Chausey; then the Jerseymen were naturally angry when the English returned to raid the Grouville beds which the authorities had only recently restocked at a cost of £4,000.

The Constable of St. Martin's could only command obedience from the English captains by turning the militia guns on them. The oyster trade remained an important one for some time, the figures for 1857 for instance showing that it still brought about £50,000 into the island.

The other main source of wealth was the tourist industry. As communications with England improved and the fares were cut in the fierce competition between the rival steamship companies, a growing surge of visitors arrived. They could cross from London, Southampton, Weymouth or Plymouth in such ships as the *Lady de Sausmarez*, 350 tons, of the British and Foreign Co.; or the *Atalanta*, 400 tons and 120 h.p. of the South of England Co., as well as by the mail steamers. French visitors came too from St. Malo or Cherbourg, and by the eighties the combined annual figures of English and French visitors had risen to some 30,000.

Guernsey, in 1815, faced a more difficult situation. The only surviving native industry was agriculture, and this was practised on family farms, some small, some minute owing to the island laws of inheritance. Yet the farmers were thrifty and hard-working, and by extensive use of vraic as a fertilizer, they created and maintained a very rich soil. On this they pastured their cattle, and by the middle of the century, helped by a ban on the import of inferior foreign breeds and by the encouragement of the Agricultural Society and its Cattle Fair, they were producing a much-improved animal. As early as 1811 Lord Braybrook had imported the first Guernsey herd into England, and twenty years later the first Guernseys entered the United States. From that time the cattle export trade held steady for 100 years, with an average annual export of 600 animals. Not that all the farmers agreed with the methods of valuation; when the 1st Herd Book, based on a points system, was brought out in 1881, an old-stager was heard to remark: 'It is not looks that count but what fills the bucket.'

The rest of the farmers' crops too were traditional, roots, grain, potatoes and broccoli. Of these grain and potatoes, both of which cropped very heavily, were exported until the forties, when the one was killed by the Repeal of the Corn Laws, and the other was hampered by a malignant potato disease.

Other crops however were in the offing. As early as 1782 a gentleman, Peter Mourant, had built a glass house to grow grapes and pines. His example was copied— a report of 1838 stated: 'The abundance of glass, reflecting the sun's rays from the roofs of the greenhouses scattered among the high clean white houses, exceeds ordinary proportions.' The building of vineries, as they were called, increased, and from this came the export of some hundreds of tons of grapes to the London market. A further stimulus came when a regular passenger and cargo steamer started to ply, daily in the summer and four days a week in the winter. Soon, in 1874, the first limited company was formed, to export grapes, early potatoes, French beans and the first semi-experimental tomatoes from 1,000 feet of heated glass. The modern glasshouse industry was born.

Meanwhile the merchant-adventurers, who had prospered so greatly in the previous century, still found a few openings, especially in the years immediately after the peace, before foreign competition had grown up again. They sent out their fast cutters on a triangular run, to Spanish and Mediterranean ports for wine, then over to South America for coffee, sugar and hides, then either back to the island for a repeat run or up to Antwerp or Hamburg for grain.

To supply and repair the ships, a local shipbuilding industry grew up in yards south and north of the Old Harbour and at St. Sampson's. Not only the carpenters and shipwrights found employment from the trade, but there were other ancillary workers, rope-makers, ship chandlers, sailmakers, caulkers, as well as the merchants of timber and provisions. In the first twenty years a hundred ships were built, full-rigged ships, barques, schooners and cutters. Then gradually steam and iron competition crushed the industry. Yet in 1864 was launched one of the fine tea-clippers, the

Golden Spur, of 656 tons, from the yard of Peter Ogier of St. Sampson's. This firm too tried to compete with the steamers by building a wooden steamer, the *Commerce*, nicknamed the *Toodley Addley*, from the extraordinary noises made by her engines. Now, a hundred years later, there are only two yards for yachts and local coasters. No wonder there was great excitement when the replacement for the marine ambulance of St. John's Brigade, the *Flying Christine II*, was built and launched at one of these.

The other outlet for the locally-built sailing ships was the granite trade. It was found that the local granite, especially the diorite or blue granite, quarried in the north-east of the island, was very durable, much more so than Scotch granite, or than the Jersey syenite, a warm reddish stone, quarried for centuries from the Mont Mado area and used in the construction of many local buildings, especially by the Jersey States. A large and increasing market for Guernsey granite arose in London and South-east England, for macadamizing road surfaces and for kerbs, granite setts and ornamental masonry. From the many quarries, which altered the whole face of the area, making it like a 'colander', according to a French visitor, the stone was taken to St. Sampson's Harbour to be crushed and then tipped straight into the ships' holds. The tonnage exported rose phenomenally, from 2,000 tons in 1810 to a 120,000 tons in 1854, and up to 458,000 tons by 1910. This remarkable expansion brought much wealth to the island, and much-needed if hard employment, and caused the population of the northern parishes to grow by over 100 per cent in thirty years. Yet a local article cast a shadow before. It reported: 'A bituminous material called Asphalt is being used experimentally in London. Should it prove successful, the stone trade will be superseded, and our only staple export be rendered comparatively valueless.'

Herm, too, had its granite quarries. These were developed by Lieut.-Colonel Lindsay, who had bought the lease of the island in 1815. His project was sound, as Herm granite was valuable, and for it he built a pier and installed machinery and a double line railway. However he lacked capital and, when the States of Guernsey refused to help him owing to a quarrel over liquor duties, he withdrew and died, bankrupt. His son-in-law, Duncan, continued his work, bringing in some 400 labourers, and for a time his granite business boomed. Then Duncan too went bankrupt and, although the quarries lingered on under new management for some years, competition from Guernsey finally killed the little island's industry.

Alderney managed to do better. There, after a bitter struggle between the Jettyites and their opponents, the Cockroaches, as the supporters of Judge Le Cocq were called, a jetty was built to handle ships at all states of the tide, and this served as the outlet for a quarry industry which flourished from 1910 until the outbreak of the Second World War.

During Duncan's time in Herm the island was visited by an optimistic mining prospector, John Hunt, who sank an experimental shaft for copper, lead and silver near Rosaire. No more successful was an English mining company which drove a shaft into the Mont Durand cliffs of Moulin Huet Bay in Guernsey. The work caused the wells and springs to dry up, and the local *chefs de famille*, led by the constables, set out to obstruct the work by legal action and other means. Wisely the English director recognized the strength of the opposition and abandoned his enterprise.

John Hunt however had already been in action in Sark, and there he found copper and silver lodes at Le Pot in Little Sark. This won him a concession from the seigneur, Peter le Pelley, and Cornish miners were brought over. But the work hung fire after Peter le Pelley was tragically drowned. His brother Edward, who succeeded him, was out rabbiting one day when a beater found a rich silver lode in the south-west cliffs of Little Sark. Getting expert advice from England, and feverish support from Guernsey and English speculators, the seigneur floated the Sark Hope Mining Company. Work went ahead, five shafts were sunk and galleries were driven in horizontally. Some silver was mined, but any income had to be used to meet the rapidly rising costs as the shafts were driven deeper. Then came disaster. The lower gallery collapsed and the sea rushed in to drown ten miners and flood the only profitable part of the mine. This finished the company with losses of over £30,000, and ruined the seigneur, who was forced to mortgage the island. Sark remained nominally in Le Pelley hands until 1852, when Mrs. Marie Collings, the daughter of the wealthy local privateer, John Allaire, foreclosed on the bond and thus became the second Dame de Sercq.

To the Sark farmers and fishermen the failure of these expectations may have appeared gloomy indeed, but there was a ray of hope. Visitors who crossed from curiosity to see the mines were attracted by the island, and Sark's tourist industry began.

With the improvements in communications and especially after the completion of the new harbour, which eliminated the necessity to land by boat, the number of visitors to Guernsey was increasing. Though it never reached the proportions of those going to Jersey, the total of passengers from England had topped the 50,000 mark by 1913. For these visitors guide-books were written, with many details of the historic buildings to be seen and the excursions to be made.

One wonders whether any visitor in the sixties, following his guide-book to the noted markets, noticed a small pile of 'love-apples' for sale. This was the name given at the time to the tomato. Local tradition recalls that originally some seeds were sent over from America, then the plants were grown in conservatories by a few farmers and horticulturalists as an experiment, producing a crop which was often brought back from the market unsold. Yet by the seventies demand had increased, and larger numbers of growers were trying tomatoes as a catch crop, down the middle of a vinery, beneath the grapes and peaches.

Further expansion was pushed by some enterprising ships'

carpenters who, finding the shipbuilding industry in decline, turned their experience to building vineries. Led by J. Poat, the first to grow tomatoes as a main crop in 1884, many far-sighted men invested in glass-houses solely for tomatoes. Some of these growers were wealthy islanders, some were English growers who came over to invest in the new industry and try their luck, but many were small men, farmers and hard-working labourers, who invested their savings in a plot of cheap land, bought the wood and glass, and by intensely hard work built up a small but thriving independent business.

Alongside the rising tomato industry and often complementary to it grew up the flower and bulb business, which was also helped and stimulated by the reasonably fast and regular steamship service to England. The Guernsey people had been well known for generations as flower-lovers and growers, but it was Charles Smith, who had converted the old Andros estate of Normanville into a famous nursery in the fifties, who started the export trade. In 1863 and 1864 he sent over consignments of camellias, daffodils and narcissi to Covent Garden. Other growers followed suit, some packing the blooms in large radish hampers in the hope of avoiding any Customs duty, and by 1904 the value of the island's flower exports had risen to £40,000. This was twice the value of the bulb exports; yet bulb growing was another useful business, most of it for island culture, but with outlets in Holland and America.

This flower and bulb export business might be a catch crop, as was the Jersey outdoor tomato crop, started about 1900, but they brought in a useful additional income to a grower or farmer who was prepared to work hard and use the advantage of a temperate and sunny climate.

The Islands then, though there were differences in detail in their development, entered the twentieth century together as stable and prosperous communities, proud of and standing firmly by their traditions, yet ready to experiment where a need or an opening appeared. Among such enterprises should be mentioned the Jersey Railway from St. Helier to St. Aubin's, and the bitter rivalry which developed between it and the motor omnibuses after 1910, the arrival of the first seaplane from St. Malo, the electric trams which clattered along between St. Peter Port and St. Sampson's, the Guernsey Telephone Company, one of the first independent telephone systems in the world, the iodine factory at Lihou, which used the local Tango as its raw material until Chilean competition forced it to close.

One thing was certain, the links with England, social, cultural, economic, were now closer than they had ever been. Denys Corbet, the schoolmaster from the Forest parish, might lament in his patois poems that the old order was changing and that the island's Gallic vernacular was dying out. But the Islands were moving with the times, and knew themselves to be small, but sturdy, bits of an Empire over which many of their fellow-islanders had scattered in the last hundred years. So, with the rest, they faced the challenge when they found that their King was at war with another enemy, not France this time, but Germany.

Chapter 11

Two World Wars and After

OF all the wars in which the Islands were involved the First World War affected them the least. This was particularly true of Jersey where, after the regular garrison was withdrawn and the militia was mobilized, life went on very much as before. There was some shortage of petrol and sugar, and some shipping losses; yet the island was regarded as so secure that a prisoner of war camp for 1,500 Germans was set up. As the war continued the labour force was spread rather thin. The Breton labourers and farmers had returned to fight for France, and of the Jerseymen, 6,500 served in the British forces. Many were volunteers, but the patriotism of the island was made even clearer by the passage through the States of the Military Service Act. This temporarily cancelled the age-old island right of not serving overseas.

A similar Act was passed in Guernsey and there it had a profounder effect. The population was 40,000 as compared with 52,000 in Jersey, and of these, besides the regulars, some 7,000 served in the war. The shortage of manpower which this caused, in addition to the many other problems, of uncertain markets, difficulties in the docks, sinkings of cargo-boats, faced the island growers especially with testing years. One employer ran a complete tomato vinery with a labour force of women.

The islanders also experienced other aspects of the war when French seaplanes had a base by Castle Cornet, and when Prince Blucher was interned as an enemy alien. He had been the tenant of Herm for over twenty years, and had lived down early criticism in the British Press and in the French, who spread a rumour that the Kaiser wanted to turn Herm into a naval base. Long before 1914 he was respected and liked by the Guernsey people, who were intrigued by his landscape gardening, tree planting and renovations.

The islanders on active service fought with many units and branches of the Army, as well as with the Royal Navy. In particular they were drafted to the Royal Irish Regiment when the Irish troubles caused its recruitment to dry up. A more ambitious policy then brought great sorrow to the Guernsey bailiwick. The Lieutenant-Governor, General Hart, put it forward that this dispersal of men meant that the island won no battle honours, and he suggested the raising of their own unit, the Royal Guernsey Light Infantry, drawn from the men of Guernsey, Alderney and Sark. This idea was followed up and the Bailiwick battalion of 1,800 men was raised and maintained. Few foresaw the risk of committing such a proportion of the manpower of a small community to one unit.

After training in Belgium they had their first taste of fire in the trenches of Passchendaele. From there they moved to take part in the successful advance with tanks at Cambrai on 20th November 1917, and were used to hold the apex of the captured salient by Masniéres. Counter-attacked by the Germans and outnumbered twenty to one, they withdrew, but twice fought back to the key village of Rue Vertes. At last, after suffering 600 casualties in two days, they were ordered to cover their brigade's withdrawal. The 'Guernseys' as they were called, had won the respect and affection of all for their marksmanship and fighting qualities. General Sir Beauvoir de Lisle, the commanding officer of the 29th Division, the 'Iron' Division, wrote to the Bailiff of Guernsey: 'I want to convey to the Guernsey authorities my very high appreciation of the valuable services rendered by the R.G.L.I. in the battle of Cambrai. Theirs was a wonderful performance.'

Later, in April 1918, the reconstituted battalion was moved swiftly to help plug the great gap driven in the British Line by Ludendorff's offensive towards Hazebrouck and the Channel ports. In this battle of the Lys, from 10th April to 14th April, they fought a bitter withdrawal action under a hail of machine-gun, mortar and artillery fire, as Ludendorff threw in all he had to batter the life out of the British Army. At Merriss they were relieved by the Australians. Less than 100 were left. As this remnant marched to entrain for duty at G.H.Q., the divisional band played them on their way.

There was pride, but also deep mourning in the homes of the Bailiwick. Many regretted General Hart's mistaken ideas of honour; to others he was anathema as a rabid teetotaller. As he left the island he pointed to a monument to a former Governor, 'I fear', he said, 'the Guernsey people will not commemorate me in that way.' 'Cheer up, sir,' was the reply. 'They will probably build a pub and call it the White Hart.'

After the Armistice and the demobilization of serving officers and men, the Islands soon returned to their normal pattern of life. There was a short period of post-war slump, particularly in Guernsey, where the States helped the unemployed by putting them to work on the construction of cliff paths. A number of islanders solved the problem by emigrating. Yet soon there followed a peaceful and prosperous era.

The overseas demand for island cattle continued to be strong, over 1,000 Jerseys and about 700 Guernseys being transhipped each year. The other main products, potatoes and tomatoes, brought a rich return to the Islands. In 1919 the value of the Jersey early potato crop was one million pounds, and the average tonnage over the years was 60,000. This business, with the growth of the outdoor tomato trade, made a firm basis for the island's economy, and was an outstanding example of skilful and careful use of the land. Only in the thirties did a threat arise, when the Colorado beetle, which had eaten its way across America, appeared in the

St. Malo area. To guard against this flying menace the Guernsey authorities instituted the spraying of their crops, but after a referendum the Jersey farmers refused to take action until a beetle was seen. When one was found in 1939 it was promptly destroyed.

In Guernsey the tomato industry steadily established itself as the island's main business. Already in 1918 the growers had a boom year, and in the years that followed a bigger and bigger acreage of glass was erected. By 1939 over 900 acres of glass-houses were in use, and the export of the crop had risen to 35,000 tons. Along with this expansion went an increasing skill in production, the average crop per plant rising steadily, and the fertility of the soil and freedom from disease being helped by artificial fertilizers and the sterilization of the soil by steam heat. The 'Rocket'-like boilers, used for this sterilization, became a familiar sight as they trundled along the island roads.

This development, coupled with the smaller expansion of the ancillary flower and bulb industry, had its side effects. A greater proportion of the island population was engaged in it, and the trades, carting, packing, box-making, which attended it. Thus it drew away labour from the already declining quarries, and reduced the volume of the traditional grape industry. Further it led to the extension of the industry to the more traditionally farming parts of the island, as the farmers naturally wanted to cash in on this profitable business, and other men looked around for a plot for a bungalow and 200 to 300 feet of glass.

This movement, allied with a rising population and rather weak control of the activities of the speculative builder, led to a sprawl of building out along the main roads, which submerged the old nucleated villages and altered the face of the interior of the island for the worse.

A similar threat to the island's beauty arose in Jersey, but there the building boom was caused by the tourist industry. The popularity of Jersey as a holiday resort was well established, and more and more visitors came over, mostly by mailboat, but from 1925 the more adventurous by flying-boat, and from 1933 by the daily service of Jersey Airways. As by 1940 the average number of visitors had risen to 200,000, hotels, boarding-houses and holiday camps had to be built to house them, besides the other amenities that holiday-makers look for. This building was largely unplanned and uncontrolled, spreading out by the beaches and along the main roads from St. Helier. Though it was suggested that some control, on the lines of the modest efforts of the Natural Beauties Committee in Guernsey, should be instituted, nothing was done, and it was left to the gallant efforts of the local National Trust to protest at spoliation and to try to secure the cliff scenery and paths for the people.

This lack of official action was strange, as one of the main developments in the Islands in this period was the growing consciousness of the States of their responsibilities to the community. In Jersey, where the islanders were so traditionally individualistic and independent, a start was made in the building up of a modern state. The Civil Service expanded to provide the permanent servants of a number of voluntary States Committees. These administered not only the island's finances, now supplemented by a small income tax, but also the schools, the hospitals and public health, the town's police, the telephone system and poor relief.

The States, too, found themselves the possessors of the castles, as ancient monuments, and in 1937 took the very important step of building the airport at St. Peter's. Yet much was still left to private enterprise and generosity. The waterworks remained a private concern until after the Second World War. Miss Barreau presented the island with a well-stocked art gallery to house paintings by such well-known local artists as Monomy, the marine artist; Philippe Jean, miniaturist; and Edmund Blampied, who has captured the Jersey scene in many a picture. Sir James Knott set an example to all with his beautiful gardens at Samares Manor. Other benefactors included Lady Trent, who redecorated St. Matthew's Church in Lalique glass, and Howard Davis, who used his fortune from South Africa to provide scholarships, an experimental farm, a hall, a park, and a lifeboat. Among this modernity the ancient things were not forgotten. The Societé Jersiaise, the island historical and archaeological society, carried out exciting excavations at La Cotte, where the discovery of the remains of Prehistoric Man, Homo Breladensis, crowned the life's work of Père Burdo of the Jesuit Order. The Societé also bravely bought the mound of the Hougue Bie, and their reward was the disclosure of the magnificent dolmen entombed there.

In Guernsey centralized control by the States, through its voluntary committees, extended a good deal further. Already before the war a number of permanent and *ad hoc* committees had evolved, permanent for Finance, Education in the Primary Schools, and appointments to the Civil Service, *ad hoc* for such concerns as the Propagation of Lobsters, and later for food control in the war. Experience in the war, the greater complexity of affairs, and perhaps the climate of opinion which led in 1920 to the increase in the number of People's Deputies to eighteen, brought a further extension of this form of government. At this time the Guernsey currency was brought into line with England, the franc being dropped as official coinage, and an income tax was imposed, administered by a committee. Another committee found itself responsible for the Island Police, a paid professional force, which took over the day-to-day police duties of the parish constables. A third new committee was entrusted with the 'nationalized' waterworks; this committee later in the thirties was to find itself involved in all the complications and arguments which led to the building of the big reservoir in St. Saviour's.

After this initial rush the development of States activities continued steadily through the years, dealing with such items as housing, pensions, workmen's compensation and harbour improvements. In the 1929 depression they were faced with the problem of unemployment; this was solved, not by a dole, but by a public works programme, the main project in which was the construction of the Val des Terres road, to link the south of the town with the heights above.

All these activities strained the island exchequer, and there were further bills ahead for the purchase of the electricity station and for the construction of the airport in the years before 1940. These two items were worth-while investments as the population rose and the number of visitors increased.

But as big a bill had been presented to the island authorities in 1923 by the English Treasury. Even before the Armistice Guernsey had contributed £100,000 towards the expenses of the war, and when peace came, the island militias were re-embodied and small English garrisons returned. It appeared that debts were paid and honour was satisfied. Then out of the blue came a demand for 'an annual contribution to the Imperial Exchequer' of £600,000 from the Islands. This demand provoked great bitterness and ill feeling, as the amount was considered quite excessive, about £222 per head for Guernsey's population, quite unfair, as the contribution from Free State Ireland had been cancelled, and lastly unconstitutional and contrary to the Islands' charters. The opposition was led by the Bailiff of Guernsey, Sir Havilland de Sausmarez, who had only two years before entertained the King and Queen to tea in his capacity as third cup-bearer. Unfortunately united action with the Jersey States was not at first possible, and they voted £400,000. However the Guernsey Bailiff, backed by the newly-elected Deputies, offered £220,000 as a final free gift. This offer was not even acknowledged and no more was heard until 1925, when a Privy Council Committee arrived to look into the affair. Ignoring most of the Bailiff's case, they blandly suggested £75,000 per annum as the island's contribution. By this time the islanders had dug their toes in, and the Bailiff, now working closely with the Jersey authorities, insisted that any contributions were a 'once for all gift'. The case was settled at last in 1927, when the Treasury accepted the 'gifts'. It had important results, for it clarified again the constitutional independence of the Islands and it ushered in a more friendly and co-operative period for the two large islands and the British Government.

In the middle of this row there arrived in Guernsey one of the more colourful Lieutenant-Governors, General Sir Charles Sackville-West. He established his official residence at the Mount, a mansion with extensive underground vaults, which had been the headquarters of John Allaire, a leading privateer in the nineteenth century. One of the General's guests there was the new Dame of Sark. She was later to marry an American, Bob Hathaway, and to take him back to the island. The official Sark reception amazed him. 'I never knew the Dame of Sark was such an important person; why, they treated you like royalty.'

Yet in Sark, too, changes were occurring. A reform of the constitution of the Court of Chief Pleas in 1922 had added twelve Deputies, elected by the other inhabitants, to the original forty tenants of the indivisible farms. The island was linked more closely to the outside world by visits from the *Courier*, the sturdy little steamer which for sixty years plied back and forth between the islands.

Another port of call of the *Courier* was Alderney, to which by this time a few visitors were penetrating, to add to the island income, an income still so dependent on agriculture, fishing and the quarries. The number of tourists grew after 1935, when the first airport in the island was established on the high southern plateau.

To Herm came no *Courier*, no aeroplane. There Sir Compton Mackenzie had settled in 1920. He delighted in the island, and stocked it with domestic animals, horses, cows, turkeys, geese and ducks. Originally, to secure privacy, he leased Jethou too, and it was to Jethou that he retreated after a few years when the Crown agents insisted on too great an expenditure on paint. Herm's next tenant, Lord Perry, a wealthy motor manufacturer satisfied them by painting all the woodwork in his racing colours, royal blue and orange.

Such were the situations in the Islands at the outbreak of

the Second World War. At first there was little material change. The more adventurous young islanders left to join up, the Jersey and Guernsey Militias and the Defence Volunteers stood on guard. Yet pacifists and others crossed over from England to safety, Jethou was advertised as a 'peaceful island to be let for the duration', and a poster of Jersey read: 'The ideal resort for wartime holidays this summer.' Little did island leaders, the decisive Bailiff Coutanche of Jersey, the elderly and kindly Bailiff Carey, the vigorous Dame of Sark, or the rather pedantic Judge French of Alderney, realize that the days and years ahead were to bring challenges, dangers, triumphs and temptations quite unimaginable in the days of the 'Phoney War'.

Then the Germans struck at Norway, Holland and Belgium and, after Dunkirk, advanced irresistibly across France. The authorities made some preparations and waited in vain for official guidance on their possible fate. Some British troops and aircraft arrived, but other troops, evacuated by the small ships of Jersey from St. Malo, passed on their way.

By the middle of June 1940 the Admiralty advised that the Islands were untenable and the British Cabinet agreed to the decision to demilitarize them. This news and the suggestion of evacuation caused considerable alarm, a rush on the banks, queues for ships and planes, and conflicting decisions. The feeling of despair was not helped by the departure of the regular troops and of the Lieutenant-Governors. In Guernsey in particular there was great heart-burning, as in ignorance of the number of ships available for evacuation, it had been decided to limit evacuation originally to children and men of fighting age. At last after two days, 5,000 children had gone. More ships arrived and the adults pushed to get on board, until the appeals of Sir John Leale and Major Sherwill calmed and steadied them. Another steadying influence was a poster, 'No place like Home. Cheer up.' The final evacuation figures were 10,000 for Jersey and 17,000 for Guernsey—roughly one in five and one in two and a half of the total populations respectively.

Meanwhile in Sark, Mrs. Hathaway, who had seen the confusion in Guernsey, called on the islanders to stay; all except thirteen did so.

In Alderney, where the enemy were only eight miles away, the decision was different. Many panic-stricken French refugees had arrived, a force of regular machine-gunners were withdrawn at twenty-four hours' notice, and the Alderney people felt themselves threatened and deserted. Judge French called a meeting of the islanders, at which he put their plight to them firmly. The decision to evacuate was almost unanimous. In response to messages, six small cargo boats arrived at last in the harbour, and by Friday, 21st June, almost the whole population had left, carrying the two suitcases they were allowed, to land safely in Weymouth. A few days later a rescue team arrived from Guernsey to deal with the cattle and pigs and the few remaining islanders.

In ironical contrast to this evacuation there arrived on the rock, Ortac, at this time the first pair of gannets, to establish in the following years two colonies of over 2,000 birds.

To deal with the threatening situation in Guernsey the government was reorganized. The Bailiff and States remained as the official government, but delegated their powers for the duration to a Controlling Committee of eight members under the presidency of Major Sherwill, the Procureur. Similar centralization was carried out in Jersey, where the Bailiff headed the Superior Council. They faced many problems if the Germans should come, chief among which were the attitude to adopt to the enemy and the danger of starvation.

Days of suspense followed. Then in the evening of Friday, 28th June, German planes attacked St. Peter Port harbour, bombing and machine-gunning the tomato lorries, and cattle and horses which had just been landed from Alderney. Other planes swept over the island, firing at haymakers and an ambulance, and attacking the lifeboat out at sea. At the same time a less fierce attack was made on St. Helier. This unprovoked attack, called in Guernsey 'The

Battle of Tomatoes', caused great bitterness. But it had another effect, the official publication by the B.B.C. of the Islands' demilitarization.

This news confirmed the Germans in their plan to invade, and in the evening of Sunday, 30th June, the first planes came in to land at Guernsey Airport. Gradually the German force built up and German orders appeared in the *Guernsey Star*. Their attitude was strict but correct, yet the islanders, ordered by their own authorities to 'offer no resistance whatever' were still dazed by the strangeness of the situation. 'It is really difficult to believe the evidence of one's eyes at seeing a German soldier on guard, to look out of one's window and see him there,' recorded one diarist. They were irked too by the evening curfew and by the withdrawal of all petrol, so that while the Germans drove everywhere they walked or rode bicycles.

The Jerseymen waited another day, until 1st July. Early in the morning a German plane dropped an ultimatum, ordering immediate surrender without resistance and as a sign the flying of white flags everywhere. Some German troops landed and the German officers gave the same orders as in Guernsey, the civil government to carry on, provided that the German Commandant agreed with their actions. Thus the island authorities found themselves in a very difficult position, forced to act as a buffer between the invaders and the islanders, and for this purpose trying to keep as much power as possible in their own hands. Yet in the early days people began to believe that their worst fears had been foolish, the Germans appeared correct and reasonable, and as one German remarked, 'This is only a temporary occupation. You must realize that the war is virtually over.'

Two days after Jersey's occupation the German Commandant in Guernsey crossed to Sark. He was met at the harbour by the Sénéschal, who walked with him up the hill to the Seigneurie. There La Dame greeted him fluently in German, and after a polite lunch he left again. Similar regulations were imposed, and a garrison of a sergeant and ten men arrived, who gradually relaxed as they grew used to the island.

There was no need for civilian regulations for Alderney. German troops occupied it from Cherbourg, and for some time the only other inhabitants were one Alderney farmer, who secured permission to take some cattle back there, and an agricultural party from Guernsey, sent over to get in the harvest and prepare for the next year.

There followed the first phase of the Occupation up to June 1941. During this time the Germans held the Islands more for prestige than for any very serious intent. A number of raids from England tested the situation. The first was a lone exploration by a Guernseyman, Hubert Nicolle. He landed from a submarine at Le Jaonnet, and after collecting information about enemy strength in men, ships and air-craft he got away. Two other Guernseymen, Mulholland and Martel, were then landed as advanced guides for a Commando raid led by Lieut.-Colonel Durnford Slater. His party came ashore at Petit Port, but, finding no Germans, could only build a road-block, cut some wires, and get away by swimming to a waiting boat. Three non-swimmers had to be left and they were rounded up. The raid was dismissed as 'a silly fiasco', though it helped to boost the island's morale. Yet to Major Sherwill it posed a problem. It was to him that Mulholland and Martel gave themselves up in their civilian clothes, and by dressing them up in old Guernsey Militia uniforms he managed to secure that the Germans treated them as prisoners of war and not as spies. Such raids by spies or soldiers on the demilitarized islands made the path of the island authorities more difficult, as they tried to walk the tight-rope between provocation and compliance.

There were many problems, the anti-Semitic laws of the Nazis, censorship of the Press and of books, suppression of the Salvation Army and of the island Freemasons, fraterniza-tion by some local girls and older women, the billeting of troops. There was sorrow too as the islanders listened to the roar of bombers, escorted by fighters from the airfields of

Jersey and Guernsey, as they left for the mass air-raids on Britain. However the islanders still had their wireless sets and the B.B.C. news helped to counteract the effect of such German reports as appeared in the Jersey *Evening Post*, that the damage was so great that the King 'had been unable to open Parliament in his golden cab'. They were heartened by R.A.F. leaflets which gave details of the raids and of the Luftwaffe losses, and enclosed a message, 'The Queen and I desire to convey to you our heartfelt sympathy in the trials you are enduring. We earnestly pray for your speedy liberation, knowing that it will surely come. George R.I.'

After August 1940, the relations between the Germans and the islanders gradually deteriorated, for the military command was separated from the civilian administration. The Commander-in-Chief was Colonel Graf von Schmettow, a cultured and fair-minded man, who waged a lengthy struggle with General Schreiber, head of the St. Germain district, the administrative area of France in which the Islands were included. Schmettow argued that 'special circumstances' should affect their handling of the Islands, and tried his best to avert full 'occupation treatment'.

Apart from their direct relations with the occupying forces, the islanders' main problem was food, both the growing of supplies for themselves and the prevention of its seizure by the Germans. In this Jersey had the advantage, as it was comparatively easy to switch from outdoor potatoes to grain, whereas the best crop from the Guernsey glass-houses turned out to be sweet corn. Yet the only hope for essential imports was France, and Raymond Falla and John Joualt left the Islands for France on a vital buying mission. Using every conceivable stratagem, including black marketeering and two sets of books, they managed to make contacts and purchases among the French; thus some supplies came in, but there was little hope of satisfying the basic needs of the people. Gradually stocks of all the main commodities grew less and less, barter was common, ingenious substitutes were tried, such as tea from blackberry, lime or rose leaves or scraped carrot, and acute shortage was to be the lot of all save a few unscrupulous ones. They said in Guernsey that the only two things which never ran short were fresh air and lavatory paper. This was supplied from the huge stocks of tomato-packing paper.

At this time the German authorities grew stricter; angered by the escape of eight men to England, they ordered all fishing boats to be concentrated in St. Peter Port. This not only hampered the activities of the fishermen, but it made escape by boat very difficult, especially for Nicolle, who had returned with a companion, Symes, on a second fact-finding mission. Their enforced stay on the island caused great complications for all who learnt of their presence, including Major Sherwill. The Germans grew very suspicious and ordered the surrender of all wireless sets as a counter-measure, and eventually, on the promise of an amnesty, of being treated as prisoners of war, Nicolle and Symes surrendered. However the German Intelligence moved in on the case, and after intensive questioning, learnt most of the facts. Nicolle, Symes and fifteen others were removed to the Cherch Midi prison in Paris, and there a little later came Sherwill too. For six months they lingered there and at last Count Von Schmettow's insistence on the terms of the amnesty prevailed, for Nicolle and Symes to pass on to a P.O.W. camp, and the rest to return to Guernsey. One man, Symes's father, did not return; it was reported that he had committed suicide in his cell.

The information that Symes had gathered did reach England. His cousin passed it and further information on via French sailors and the Maquis to the British agent in Spain. Eventually the Gestapo caught the cousin, who was taken away from the island to prison after prison, until he arrived, one of the first Channel Islanders, in Buchenwald.

Sherwill's position as President of the Controlling Committee was taken over by Jurat Sir John Leale, an ascetic and idealist, and a clear-headed leader. His policy in dealing with the Germans was unlimited patience and absolute insistence on the strict letter of The Hague Convention. As he said later, 'We espoused The Hague Convention for better, for worse.' The terms of The Hague Convention were the basis too of Bailiff Coutanche's policy in Jersey, but in Sark things were handled differently. Mrs. Hathaway simply dominated the Germans, using such remarks as: 'But you can't do that, I won't allow it,' or 'Oh, dear, no, that's not the way the British do things; in Britain we never shout.'

For a period after the Battle of Britain the Islands were in a backwater of the war. The islanders' main concern was food, yet manifestations of resistance appeared periodically, to stir the Germans into feverish activity and to embarrass the official position of the island authorities. Great sorrow was felt in Jersey over the execution there by shooting of François Scornet, the young French leader of a group who sailed to join the Free French but mistakenly landed in Guernsey. Some amusement was felt over minor acts of sabotage, such as the cutting of telephone wires. But much bitterness and criticism was aroused by official condemnation of those islanders who expressed their pent-up feelings of loyalty by chalking up 'V' signs.

After the German attack on Russia the situation on the Islands changed dramatically. The decision was taken to construct the Atlantic Wall, and in that immense scheme of fortification the Channel Islands were to be especially important, particularly in Hitler's eyes. He felt certain that for prestige purposes Britain would attempt to regain them, and he ordered that work should be pushed ahead to turn them into an impregnable fortress.

In the years that followed this policy was carried to almost incredible lengths, so much so that the German officers who opposed Hitler's obsession, referred to it as his 'Island Madness', saying that he had put the Islands 'under a glass case'. Thousands of troops were brought over, masses of artillery, shiploads of cement, and large numbers of the foreign labourers in the Todt organization. The effect was to ring the Islands with the most formidable fortifications, and to pin down some 36,000 men, whose presence elsewhere would have been of vital assistance to the German High Command later in the war.

These defence systems had of course their physical effect on the Islands, mainly ugly and damaging. Alderney, in particular, was turned into a compact fortress, with a fire-control system like a battleship. Great tunnels were bored underground for ammunition, and in Jersey and Guernsey extensive underground hospitals were constructed to take between 600 and 800 beds.

For all this building some 18,000 foreign workers, drawn from many nations, were brought over to the Islands. Their life was grim indeed, housed like animals, half-starved or worse, driven to work before daylight and returning in the dark. Those islanders who lived near the Todt prisons had to get used to the screams, and it was a common sight to see the pitiable men wading in the sewer discharge on the chance of food scraps. Many acts of surreptitious kindness were done, none more than by Dr. McKinstry, the Jersey Medical Officer of Health, who provided faked ration books and identity cards for those who did succeed in escaping. No one however could help the foreign workers in Alderney. With vitually no witnesses it can only be guessed what nameless cruelties were suffered by the Todt workers, or by the inhabitants of the concentration camps in the island. The prisoners in their blue-and-white-striped pyjama uniforms could be seen as they left for work, and the tall barbed-wire fences and the kennels for Alsatian dogs were just visible from the airfield. The situation was summed up in the words of a Frenchwoman, a cook in one of the Todt camps, 'Alderney, isle of silence, of nightmare and of terror.'

With the conversion of the Islands into important fortresses, there were certain natural consequences. Firstly some of the more daring islanders tried to gather and get out information for Allied Intelligence. The most effective were the group of Jerseymen run by Major Crawford-Morrison, the A.R.P. Controller. They gathered precise information of all the German military locations; this was mapped and the result photographed down to postage stamp size, and eventually, when Major Morrison was deported, he managed to get a copy back to England.

Secondly, as the Germans feared attack, the islanders were controlled more closely by such actions as the attempted confiscation of all wireless sets, and after the Dieppe raid, by the destruction of all houses overlooking the gun positions. Then, in September 1942, Hitler himself ordered that anyone born in England should be deported to internment camps in Germany. Precise numbers were laid down, 1,200 for Jersey and 800 for Guernsey, which were adhered to, in spite of the apologies of the local commanders. This sudden uprooting caused great suffering and sorrow, and led, in Jersey, to public demonstrations, in which the deportees and the onlookers joined in shouting 'Churchill, England, Jersey'.

The third development was raiding by the Commandos, now much more experienced than in the early Guernsey raids. Guided by Major Appleyard, who used the local knowledge of a Guernsey seaman, Bonny Newton, a Commando unit first struck at the Casquets, taking seven prisoners. Then after an unsuccessful raid on Cherbourg, they landed in Sark, where they caught five Germans asleep. After losing four of the struggling, kicking men in the darkness, they got away with one prisoner, and with up-to-date information on the conditions in the Islands. The German reaction was immediate, the doubling of guards, an earlier curfew, the deportation of anyone who had ever held the King's Commission, and the chaining of Dieppe prisoners as a reprisal for the bound wrists of the captured men. Hitler's own reaction was more extreme, for he ordered that 'all Commandos should be slaughtered to the last man'.

In spite of these highlights of excitement or sorrow or fear, for most islanders these years meant a monotonous routine, restrictions, and scarce and dreary food. The increasing shortage of food and other supplies, while it stimulated many examples of inventiveness, had a serious effect on the people's health; men and women grew more lethargic, their memories often failed. However skilfully the chemists might strive to supplement their stock with clandestine French imports or ingenious substitutes, the basic fact remained that the islanders were gravely undernourished. The situation was not helped when in April 1943 the German Command ordered a severe ration cut as a reprisal for R.A.F. attacks on German cargo boats. The two bailiffs protested vigorously against this, as a breach of The Hague Convention, and eventually the ration was restored.

Yet there were consolations, especially after the German defeat in North Africa. Many of the occupying troops realized that the war was being lost. General Muller, the fiery disciplinarian, and the more experienced units were sent to the Russian front, Von Schmettow regained his position as Commander-in-Chief. Further encouragement came to the people of Guernsey and Sark from copies of G.U.N.S., the Guernsey Underground News Service. This secret news-sheet was started by Charles Machon, who typed out copies, at one time a hundred a day, from news brought to him by his four assistants.

Eventually the Germans, helped by an informer, picked up his trail, and after trial he was taken to Potsdam Prison where he died. One assistant also died in prison, but three others, Falla, Legg, and Duquemin were sent on the long grim journey, from prison to prison, until they reached a concentration camp. These terrible places housed a number of islanders, gathered in for various reasons—possession of a wireless set, assistance to the Todt workers, minor acts of sabotage. There some died and others suffered like all the inmates. As the Jerseyman, Le Druillenec, an inmate of Belsen, said afterwards, 'I learnt how hard it is to destroy the human body. I saw men in indescribable agony, whose only wish was to die quickly, but they would go on, hour after hour, showing by their eyes or by some twitch of their limbs that there was still life left.'

The third phase of the war for the Islands started with the invasion of Normandy. It was preceded by a number of air attacks on the Islands, to knock out the German radar installations, and then on the night of 5th June 1944, the islanders lay awake as they heard wave after wave of planes pass by overhead. There followed the D Day landings and the reconquest by the Allies of the Cotentin and the St. Malo area. To Hitler, with his obsession, it seemed clear that the British would attack the Islands, and he gave orders that they were to be defended to the last. General Jodl was more realistic. He had already anticipated that the Allies would by-pass the Islands, and would try to starve out the garrisons; for this reason he had evacuated the survivors from the concentration camps and the Todt workers.

Only gradually did their situation dawn on the islanders themselves. At first, buoyed up by the landings and the German withdrawal, they hoped for an early release. Like many experts, they underestimated the fighting tenacity of the retreating German forces. They also found themselves in June 1944 with a new German naval commander, Vice-Admiral Huffmeier, a rabid Nazi, who was inspired by Admiral Doenitz with the theory of 'fanatical resistance' and who aimed to supplant Von Schmettow as Commander-in-Chief.

From this time the islanders were cheered in spirit by the news from the powerful B.B.C. Forces transmitter, which they picked up on home-made crystal sets. In the manufacture of these, Father Rey, of the Jesuit College in Jersey, held the record, sixty-three sets. For the more adventurous there was the challenge of escaping from Jersey to France; this challenge was accepted by fifty-nine young Jersey men and women, of whom forty-seven reached France safely.

However the islanders' bodies were being starved, not only by the Germans, who had little food themselves, but by the British Admiralty on Churchill's orders. He insisted that the Germans were solely responsible for the food supplies of the countries they occupied.

To save his people Alexander Coutanche moved heaven and earth. He protested strongly to the German Command and ensured that copies of his protest reached Whitehall via France. He even suggested that he should sail under a safe conduct to London to explain the situation. Little success attended his efforts at first, as Von Schmettow dismissed curtly any suggestion of a German surrender, and disclaimed any responsibility for supplying the populations. In fact there was a threat of worse to come; a directive from Supreme Headquarters in Berlin stated that civilian rations were to be reduced to the barest survival level and if necessary, the entire civilian population, except for able-bodied men, were to be 'pushed over to the enemy'. An ominous phrase.

The agent of relief was Fred Noyon, a Guernsey fisherman. The details of the situation were entrusted to him, and with a companion he slipped away in his boat on 3rd November. Covered by a drizzle, he sailed up Channel, where he was intercepted by an American submarine chaser and taken into Cherbourg. From there his papers reached London. The information convinced the authorities, and permission was granted by the Germans for the bailiffs to get in touch with the Red Cross.

Weeks passed, conditions grew worse, and disappointments were many; but at last two days after a very bare Christmas the Red Cross ship *Vega* reached Guernsey. There and in Sark and Jersey began the distribution of food parcels, one per person. The islanders gazed in delighted amazement at items they had forgotten, real tea, real biscuits, cheese, and tinned meat.

The parcels undoubtedly helped, but, as the weeks went by, starvation was very close for most islanders, and close too for the German troops. They were seen rummaging in dustbins, or searching for limpets or nettles. The living conditions were made even worse by the almost complete exhaustion of all supplies of fuel for heating or light.

In the meantime Vice-Admiral Huffmeier had been intriguing with those who were highest in Hitler's favour, and in February 1945, he gained his reward. He replaced Von Schmettow as Commander-in-Chief of the Channel Islands. The islanders now found themselves controlled by a man who declared that 'I have only one aim, to hold out until final victory'. Ironically his confidence and his reputation were increased by the success of a raid planned by Von Schmettow. This raid was carried out on Granville in Normandy by German volunteers, who caught the Americans unawares and brought back to Jersey twenty-six prisoners. Under such a man the islanders' rejoicings as they learnt of the Allied advances were tempered by fear of what might yet be in store for them. Among the rumours one thing was certain; Huffmeier was determined to hold out even if the war ended and to keep the Islands as a bargaining counter. Even though there was an assassination plot among his subordinates and a vague plan for a general mutiny among the troops, even though Hitler was dead and the war was virtually over, Huffmeier held to his fanatic plan, which would have meant either mass destruction in the Islands or mass starvation.

At last, on 8th May, the Bailiff of Guernsey and Sir John Leale were summoned to the German H.Q., to be told that the war was over, and for the Islands too. Out came the Union Jacks, and in Jersey, where Churchill's speech was relayed in Royal Square, a great cheering crowd surrounded Bailiff Coutanche as he came down from the balcony to mingle with the people.

Even then Huffmeier quibbled with Brigadier Snow, the commander of the Liberation Force, over the terms of surrender, and it was not until the early morning of Wednesday, 9th May, that the surrender documents were signed.

With the Liberation many problems faced the island

authorities and the British forces, problems of dealing with the German prisoners, food shortage, the abandoned concrete defences, mines and wire, the evacuated islanders so eager to return home. Some 20,000 German prisoners were taken away to England and British troops came in to clear up the debris. King George and Queen Elizabeth sailed to the Islands. Whitehall officials arrived, with advice, with a large grant to redeem the worthless Occupation marks, and with a low-interest loan to help the States meet their debts. The children returned, many with strange accents, picked up in Scotland or the North of England. George Dawson appeared to buy up for scrap the steel from the German fortifications.

Amid the excitement and rejoicing there arose demands for revenge on those who were known or thought to have collaborated with the enemy. Against such a witch-hunt the authorities wisely stood firm; in this they were supported by a statement in the House of Commons from the Home Secretary, Mr. Chuter Ede. He said, 'The Channel Islands have every reason to be proud of themselves and we have every reason to be proud of them. That after a period of great suffering there should have been a tendency in certain quarters, not fully informed of all the facts, to indulge in recriminations is not surprising; but I hope, in the interests of the future of the Islands, nothing will be said in this House to encourage any such tendency.'

Any recriminations were soon to be forgotten in the tasks of reconstruction. The seed potatoes were planted, the tomato plants were pricked out, the hoteliers pressed the wholesalers for the necessities to refurnish and restock the hotels, and the shopkeepers and stores availed themselves of the fact that the Islands were for a time on the United Kingdom's Export Market.

The effort paid dividends, and by 1947 the larger islands had regained the standards of prosperity they had enjoyed before the war, and had hopes of an even better state. With the demand for food there was a big market for their products. Jersey sent away over 24,000 tons of potatoes, and nearly 29,000 tons of tomatoes in 1946, and the demand from Great Britain, America and the Dominions for her cattle was so great that for eight years the annual export averaged 2,000 animals.

It took a little longer to restore Guernsey's heated glass-house industry, but by 1947 the export of 12 lb. chips of tomatoes had topped the seven million mark, and her cattle too were sent overseas, 835 of them.

Those in the Jersey tourist industry were relieved to find that their English visitors had not forgotten them, for some 224,000 holiday-makers, moved by memories or curiosity about the Occupation or by advertisements, came over. Somewhat to the surprise of the Guernseymen over 67,000 visitors came to their island too, a 50 per cent increase on the pre-war figure.

This external interest spurred the islanders to further efforts to remove or conceal the concrete disfigurements left by the Germans and to restore amenities, such as the golf-course at L'Ancresse, and at Grouville, where the great Harry Vardon had been born and learnt his game.

At this time the States of Guernsey took the opportunity of buying the island of Herm, to let it to a new tenant, Jeffries, with the proviso that islanders and visitors from Guernsey should be able to enjoy its beauty and peace. After two years Major Wood succeeded to the tenancy and further improvements and developments followed.

A much more formidable task of reconstruction faced Brigadier French and the people of Alderney. They were destined to return to a desolated island of barbed wire and concrete bunkers, derelict houses, ruined quarries and waste farms. The reconstruction was undertaken as a planned operation, heavily subsidized by the British Government. Parties of islanders returned as and when houses were available for them, and tackled the reclamation of the land on a communal basis. Guernsey cattle were brought over to rebuild the herds, market gardening was started, a trickle of tourists came over, and by 1947 the islanders had begun to stand again on their own feet.

In the following year the island's economy was further diversified by the establishment of a meat-packing station and a silencer factory. But these ventures did not last, and Alderney fell back for a living on agriculture, market-gardening and fishing, helped out by exports of shingle-gravel, and the income which came from visitors and a growing number of well-to-do residents, among them the picturesque personality, T. H. White, the author.

During this period of island recovery, a movement grew in intensity, which had had its roots in pre-war opinions and was fanned by some criticism of official leadership during the Occupation. This movement called for reform of the constitutions of the Islands, and fitted in with the views of the British Government. The States of Jersey and of Guernsey made official moves to learn the King's pleasure, and as a result a Committee of the Privy Council, headed by Viscount Samuel, was appointed to visit the Islands and, after careful and tactful inquiries, to make recommendations for reform. The Committee's proposals were not wholly acceptable to the Islands, but in the main they were passed as Island Laws with very important results.

Dealing with the Royal Courts, the Judiciary, they laid down that in future the jurats should be judges of fact and not of law, which was to be the sole responsibility of each bailiff. They also recommended that in due course a Court of Appeal for the Channel Islands should be set up, in the Islands. This recommendation was not however carried into effect until 1964, when a court was established, consisting of the two bailiffs and a panel of English judges.

When they dealt with the future composition of the Island States, they laid down that the jurats and the rectors should no longer be members, and that the number of popularly elected Deputies should be increased, in Jersey to twenty-eight and in Guernsey to thirty-three. The twelve Jersey Constables, elected from the parishes, were retained in the

Assembly, as were the Guernsey Douzaine Representatives, though their number was reduced to ten. These changes ensured that the directly elected representatives were a majority of each body, but to ensure continuity and a measure of experience twelve Senators in Jersey and twelve Conseillers in Guernsey were to be added, through election by a reformed type of Electoral College.

More far-reaching still was the reform of the Alderney constitution, carried out a year later, in 1948. The complete breach with the past in the Occupation gave an opening for virtually all feudal relics to be swept away. The Alderney Court, a purely judicial body, emerged with a Chairman and six Jurats, appointed by the Home Secretary. The Legislature, the States of Alderney, was to consist of a President, elected triennially, and nine Deputies, elected by universal suffrage, with no bar of sex or property, and only twelve months' residential qualification.

At the same time the Alderney people had to face the realities of their difficult economic situation, and for the time being agreed that the Guernsey authorities should take on responsibility for their finance, and for the police, the airport, education and the social services. In return Alderney undertook to pay the same taxes as in Guernsey, and to send Deputies to attend the relevant meetings of the Guernsey States.

In the period from 1948 these reforms had considerable, if varied, effects on the Islands. In Jersey their impact was to give an opening to a number of shrewd and efficient business brains. A firm basis for the activities of these leaders was provided by the flourishing, or perhaps one should say booming, state of the island economy. Every year the tourist industry expanded, the number of visitors rising to above the half-million mark in 1964. To cater for them there was a big expansion in the number and in the size of hotels, and every effort was made by the Tourist Committee, under a law of 1948, to see that the accommodation offered was suitable, and to provide the necessary attractions.

The finance for this big expansion came not only from island sources, but also from outside investments. They, along with finance houses, investment trusts and merchant banks, were attracted by the island's tax position and the invisible exports which thus accrued were a further valuable addition to Jersey's finances.

During the same period the Jersey farmers prospered too. It is true that they faced an annual threat from the pest, the Colorado beeetle, yet any invaders were promptly dealt with. The individual farmer was backed in this battle by assistance from the States, which had become an original member of the European Plant Protection Organization. As a result of these precautions and of the farmers' intensive skilled cultivation, the tonnage of produce exported rose steadily, the total approaching 80,000 tons in 1963. In this total there was some change of emphasis through the years, with a drop in the outdoor tomato crop, a rise in early potatoes, and a big expansion in the growing of flowers and broccoli. At the same time the Jersey Herd, while it declined a little in numbers and did not maintain the high export figures of the immediate post-war years, still averaged from 500 to 800 exported, its customers ranging from the U.S.A. to Jugoslavia and Turkey, with inquiries pending from the U.S.S.R.

Using public loans and the income raised by taxes from this prosperity, the various States Committees worked energetically to extend and modernize in the areas which were their particular concern. A big public housing programme was got under way. Further building was done for the Education Department, which had a heavy task to make adequate provision at primary and secondary level for the great majority of the island's children, up to a standard equivalent to the requirements of the Butler Act.

Much more controversial was the Insurance Act of 1951. The passage of this measure, which included a contributory scheme for pensions for Old Age and Widows, Sickness and Accident, as well as grants for Maternity and Death, and children's allowances, provoked much unrest in the country parishes. Violent and inflammatory speeches were made, supporters of the measure were chased and vilified. But after it had been in operation for a time, the resistance faded, and the social justice and the benefits were recognized.

To its opponents it savoured of Socialism, but it did not approach Beveridge's proposals. Although entry to hospital was later made free if required, the island was not prepared to accept a Health Service, nor was there unemployment pay.

Such were some of the main threads in Jersey's story during this time. Other highlights, of more glamour or excitement, included visits by Elizabeth as Princess and as Queen, with the Duke of Edinburgh, and the visit of Elizabeth, the Queen Mother, for the eighteenth Liberation anniversary, the grant of a life peerage to Alexander Coutanche on his retirement, the successful revivals of the Battle of Flowers, appearances by professional racing drivers, such as B. Bira, in the island road races, and the establishment by Gerald Durrell of his zoo at Les Augres Manor.

Another event of lasting significance for good or bad was the construction, at Les Platons, of the great TV mast, which served to link the Islands with British broadcasting and later for the dissemination of the Island's commercial network, Channel TV.

The Bailiwick of Guernsey was honoured by the royal visitors too, in particular in 1949, when Princess Elizabeth and the Duke of Edinburgh paid Sark the first royal visit for nearly fifty years. He opened La Maseline Harbour, the new jetty which provided much better facilities for passenger and cargo boats than the little Creux Harbour round the headland. Guernsey had other memorable events, the launching of the *Flying Christine* ambulance, the appointment of a new bailiff, Sir William Arnold, the maiden visit of R.M.S. *Sarnia*, the new British Railways steamer, which with the *Caesarea* was to be the Islands' main sea link with Britain, the award of the R.N.L.I. Gold Medal to the lifeboat coxswain, Captain Petit, and the promotion of the first deep-sea hydrofoil passenger service in the *Condor I*.

Another pioneering enterprise was undertaken by the States Water Board, when, as a security against drought, they installed a sea-water distillation plant, with a capacity in emergency of 20,000 gallons per hour. This matched in initiative the Gas Board's conversion of their plant to produce butane gas, and in foresight the construction in Jersey of a sewage processing plant, to render the waste materials into a compost suitable for use on the island's farms.

Yet, on the whole, in the post-Reform period, the pace of Guernsey's development was less hot, less professional. The island prospered with a steady rise in tomato exports until 1961. The industry's efficiency was increased with the help of the Experimental Station and the Advisory Service, and through the overall control of the Marketing Board, with its bulk packing station and its introduction of palletization, whereby tomato-trays, wired together in blocks, could be handled more easily on boat and train. The later drop in tomato figures was balanced by rising exports of flowers, grown outdoors or under glass. The total of boxes in 1963 reached above the two million mark.

The tourist industry also grew steadily, aided by improved communications, advertisement, and personal recommendation, and the more or less constant annual increase of visitors by 7 per cent had brought the total for 1964 up to the region of 180,000.

Against these impressive figures must be balanced other facts. The island's grape industry was in decline, only two quarries survived as going concerns, the bulb industry was hampered by disease, and the farmers faced a difficult time. Although the States Dairy, first established to cope with the demands of the Germans, provided a useful marketing centre for milk, butter and cream, the island herd decreased in numbers, the total of cattle exported dropped to an infinitesimal figure, and there was a serious shortage of pasture.

One reason for this was the demand for land for building, not only to house islanders in their own homes or in States-built estates, but also for those who came over from England or other parts to retire. In spite of strict control of house sales, and the emigration of many younger people, the population had risen to over 45,000 in 1961, a high density in view of the size of the island, a mere 25 square miles.

To provide for this population the Education Department built up a schools system on the standard Butler Act lines, and the Insurance Authority planned Social Security services which should approach those offered in Jersey. In this they met strong opposition from the Guernseymen; a hostile petition signed by 14,000 was presented, and the scheme had to be shelved for thirteen years, until it was reconstituted with some additional unemployment and health benefits.

The same success was not gained by another petition from 10,000 people who protested against the sale of the Fort George area to an English development company. It was indeed difficult to decide what use to make of such derelict War Department property and land, as the Jersey States found in their discussions of the future of Fort Regent.

All in all at the end of this era, though the Islands were busy and prosperous, the communities were faced by many problems, among them foreign competition, the possibility of the Common Market, disruption of their vital communications by English strikers, rising populations and the fear that the sun might not shine next year.

Yet in their long history they had faced many problems over the centuries. A quotation from the war-time study of the situation of the Islands, entitled *Nos Isles*, may well bring this story to its conclusion.

'Loyalty to the Crown, a sturdy independence of character, a strong attachment to self-government, a remarkable capacity for adaptation to changing economic conditions; these great virtues will provide the foundations on which the edifice of the future happiness and prosperity of the Islands can safely rest.'

List of Books

The Channel Islands E. Carey, 1924
The Mediaeval Administration of the Channel Islands 1199–1399 Professor J. H. Le Patourel, 1937
Channel Islands & Newfoundland C. R. Fay, 1961
Methodism in the Channel Islands R. D. Moore, 1952
Nos Isles C. I. Study Group, 1944
Archaeology of the Channel Islands Vol I T. D. Kendrick Vol II J. Hawkes, 1937
A History of the Island of Jersey G. R. Balleine, 1950
The Bailiwick of Jersey G. R. Balleine
Gorey Castle Official Guide N. V. L. Rybot, 1949
Jersey under the Swastika R. Mollet, 1945
Bulletins of the Societé Jersiaise
Guernsey F. R. Tupper, 1876
Guernsey V. Coysh, 1960
Essays on Guernsey History E. Carey, 1936
The Guernsey Farmhouse Members of the Guernsey Society, 1963
Guernsey Folklore Sir E. Maccullough, 1903
Alderney Official Guide A. H. Ewen & others, 1961
Dame of Sark S. Hathaway, 1961
Sark M. Marshall, 1961
The Story of Sark A. R. de Carteret, 1956
Herm M. Marshall, 1958
Islands in Danger A. & M. Wood, 1955
Transactions of the Societé Guernsiaise
The Bailiwick of Guernsey C. P. Le Huray, 1952

Index

J = *Jersey;* *G* = *Guernsey*